SERGEI O. PROKOFIEFF (1954–2014) studied Fine Arts and Painting at the Moscow School of Art. He encountered the work of Rudolf Steiner in his youth, and soon decided to devote his life to it. He became active as an author and lecturer in 1982, and helped found the Anthroposophical Society in his native Russia in 1991. In Easter 2001, he was appointed as a member of the Executive Council of the General Anthroposophical Society in Dornach, Switzerland, on which he served until his death. A popular speaker, he authored numerous books and articles that are published in many languages.

I0808417

Books by Sergei O. Prokofieff from Temple Lodge Publishing:

Anthroposophy and The Philosophy of Freedom
The Appearance of Christ in the Etheric
Crisis in the Anthroposophical Society and Pathways to the Future (with Peter Selg)
The Cycle of the Seasons and the Seven Liberal Arts
The Cycle of the Year as a Path of Initiation
The East in the Light of the West, Parts One to Three
The Encounter with Evil and its Overcoming through Spiritual Science
The Esoteric Significance of Spiritual Work in Anthroposophical Groups
Eternal Individuality, Towards a Karmic Biography of Novalis
The Foundation Stone Meditation
The Guardian of the Threshold and The Philosophy of Freedom
The Heavenly Sophia and the Living Being Anthroposophia
May Human Beings Hear It!, The Mystery of the Christmas Conference
The Mystery of John the Baptist and John the Evangelist
The Mystery of the Resurrection in the Light of Anthroposophy
The Occult Significance of Forgiveness
Prophecy of the Russian Epic
Relating to Rudolf Steiner
Rudolf Steiner and the Founding of the New Mysteries
Rudolf Steiner's Path of Initiation
Rudolf Steiner's Research into Karma
Rudolf Steiner's Sculptural Group
The Spiritual Origins of Eastern Europe and the Future Mysteries of the Holy Grail
The Twelve Holy Nights and the Spiritual Hierarchies
What is Anthroposophy?
The Whitsun Impulse
Why Become a Member of the Anthroposophical Society?
Why Become a Member of the School of Spiritual Science?

The Case of Valentin Tomberg
Valentin Tomberg, Rudolf Steiner and Anthroposophy

THE ENCOUNTER WITH EVIL

AND ITS OVERCOMING THROUGH SPIRITUAL SCIENCE

with Essays on
The Foundation Stone

SERGEI O. PROKOFIEFF

TEMPLE LODGE
London

Translated from Russian by Simon Blaxland de Lange

Temple Lodge Publishing
51 Queen Caroline Street
London W6 9QL

www.templelodge.com

Published by Temple Lodge 1999
Reprinted 2001

Chapters 1 and 2 have previously been published in German as *Die Begegnung mit dem Bösen und seine Überwindung in der Geisteswissenschaft, Der Grundstein des Guten* (1999) and *Die Mysterien der Hirten und der Könige im Lichte der Anthroposophie* (1998) respectively, both by Verlag am Goetheanum, Dornach, Switzerland. Chapter 3 was included in the collection *Wege zur Christus-Erfahrung* (1991), also published by Verlag am Goetheanum

A catalogue record for this book is available from the British Library

ISBN 1 902636 10 4

Cover by S. Gulbekian. Cover sketch by Anne Stockton, based on part of the 'Red Window' at the Goetheanum, Dornach, Switzerland
Typeset by DP Photosetting, Aylesbury, Bucks.
Printed and bound by 4Edge Ltd., Essex

Contents

Foreword

The present volume consists of essays which represent transcripts of lectures given on different occasions.

The first part of the volume contains two lectures which I gave in 1998 in Switzerland, Russia, the Czech Republic and Germany. Their content reflects the attempt to enter, with the help of spiritual science, into the deeper, esoteric foundations of the principal events of the twentieth century which is now coming to an end, characterised as it has been by phenomena of evil hitherto without precedent in human history.

This first part is concluded by a presentation of certain elements of the esoteric work which is possible within the Anthroposophical Society and also of perspectives of development arising out of this work for the anthroposophical movement as a whole, as these can be discerned on the threshold of the new millennium. These perspectives are directly associated with the main task of the fifth post-Atlantean period, a task which—according to Rudolf Steiner—consists in getting to know the forces of evil at work in earthly evolution, inasmuch as in such knowledge is already contained the beginning of their gradual overcoming.

In order that this central task of the present epoch might be fulfilled, at the Christmas Conference of 1923 Rudolf Steiner imparted to the members of the newly founded Anthroposophical Society the *Foundation Stone of the Good*, which is intended to live in the hearts and souls of anthroposophists as a firm foundation for their esoteric work and also as a source of those inner forces through which the task referred to above can be accomplished. For the mystery of the Foundation Stone consists in its capacity to lead every human being who lays it in his heart to a conscious experience of the principal *spiritual* event of our time—the appearance of Christ in an etheric form. This is possible because the Foundation Stone was created by Rudolf Steiner out of the etheric forces deriving directly from the Sun kingdom of the Christ, who is the central source of all impulses of good in our cosmos.

The second part of the book is likewise devoted to the theme of the etheric advent and its connection with the Foundation Stone of the Christmas Conference. It consists of the transcripts of two earlier lectures already published in German by Verlag am Goetheanum. These are concerned with *further* aspects of this central event in connection with the present tasks of the anthroposophical movement and the spiritual essence of the Foundation Stone.

This inner relationship of both lectures with the content of the first part—despite the wholly different approach to the theme—has also made it possible to include them in the present volume.

Sergei O. Prokofieff
London, June 1999

ONE

The Encounter with Evil and its Overcoming through Spiritual Science

The Foundation Stone of the Good

'What people of the fifth post-Atlantean epoch must learn to recognise is the fully conscious struggle against the evil rising up in the evolution of humanity.'

Rudolf Steiner, 18 November 1917

Anyone who looks in an unprejudiced way at modern civilisation as it has developed by the end of our century will be able without difficulty to discern the main reasons for its precipitous collapse in the ever intensifying forces of death and evil with which it is beset.

The former kind of forces have in our time taken hold of virtually all areas of human life, for never in the entire history of humanity on Earth has the danger of total physical annihilation been so evident a threat. The possibility of a total nuclear catastrophe, the irreparable pollution of the environment, the new illnesses caused by the invasion of materialistic science into realms directly connected with the very foundations of man's earthly existence (genetic engineering, cloning etc.), not to speak of the epidemics of abortions and the approaching universal legalisation of euthanasia ('humanitarian' death)—all this makes it clearly apparent that the forces of death have become dominant in all areas of modern civilisation and are pushing it towards an abyss.

Another abyss approaches modern mankind from within. It is given its character by forces of a different kind which have also appeared in our century with a hitherto unprecedented power. These are the forces of evil. Never has such a multiplicity of infernal forces invaded the world through the souls of human beings. Two world wars, the Bolshevik and Nazi extermination camps, the genocide of entire peoples and much, much else besides—all these things speak of how the working of the forces of evil in their assault upon the human soul has in the twentieth century risen to a new, qualitatively different level.

Only a deeper knowledge of what is taking place today in the world such as springs from the sources of esoteric Christianity can help us to explain to present-day humanity the true reasons for this unprecedented strengthening of the death-forces outside and the evil forces within the human soul. The main representative of esoteric Christianity in our time is Anthroposophy or spiritual science, founded at the beginning of the twentieth century by Rudolf Steiner. For in the true mysteries of the living Christ, which spiritual science proclaims to the world, we find an answer to both the principal questions which now stand in all their terrifying and growing dimensions before mankind: the question of death and the question of evil.

An answer to the first question can be found in a real

understanding of the Mystery of Golgotha as a unique divine Deed on the Earth, as a result of which the possibility of overcoming death was introduced for the first time into earthly evolution. From the thirteenth century onwards, all true Rosicrucians have laboured in the circles of esoteric Christianity at the task of unveiling the death-transcending resurrection-forces in the human soul, a task which they call working on the 'philosopher's stone'.

An answer to the second question is given by the repetition of the Mystery of Golgotha in the supersensible worlds, of which Anthroposophy speaks out of the sources of spiritual research.[1] The chief consequence of this event in the higher worlds is the new appearance of Christ to mankind, though this time not in a physical but in a supersensible form—the beginning of which revelation falls in our twentieth century.

This new revelation of Christ from the all-encompassing sphere of the life (etheric) forces of the Earth is—according to spiritual science—the central spiritual event of our time. It is, moreover, connected in a very direct way with the possibility that human beings have of transforming evil into good in the sense of a rightly understood Manichean principle.

The two central occult streams of esoteric Christianity, the Rosicrucian and the Manichean, have in our time found their synthesis and their modern expression—appropriate for the present epoch of the consciousness soul—in spiritual science.

In this connection, in a lecture of 25 October 1918,[2] Rudolf Steiner unfolded the mystery of the interrelationship and collaboration of the forces of death and the forces of evil in earthly evolution over the course of three post-Atlantean epochs: the Graeco-Latin, the modern ('European') and the future Slavic epoch. Thus, according to his spiritual-scientific research, the death-forces reached their apogee in the inner nature of the human soul in the fourth, Graeco-Latin epoch. It was therefore also at that time that the Mystery of Golgotha took place, where the death-forces were counterbalanced by resurrection-forces which overcame them.

In the next epoch, in which we are now living, the death-forces have taken another direction—from within outwards. Hence it is our time which sees their apogee in outer civilisation, whereas in the human soul itself a new temptation is appearing ever more strongly, the temptation by the forces of evil. Finally, after our 'European' epoch and in approximately 1500 years there will follow the next, sixth or 'Slavic' epoch. This will be a time when new clairvoyant faculties will spread throughout mankind, and through such a direct relationship with the spiritual world human beings will gradually be able to overcome the death-forces which have taken hold of modern civilisation, with the help of forces having their origin in the Mystery of Golgotha.

Simultaneously with this, the forces of evil which in our fifth post-Atlantean epoch are manifesting themselves increasingly in the depths of the human soul will also find their path outwards (similarly to the death-forces in the previous epoch). There will then necessarily be a battle with this 'objective' evil on the magical plane, with the power of white magic opposing its black-magical energies. The source of this white magic will be the conscious clairvoyant relationship of human beings with the etheric Christ. This process will reach its culmination in the seventh, 'American' epoch.

However, the first steps in forming such a direct relationship with Christ must be taken already in our epoch. For what will manifest only in the future is being prepared today, which means that it must above all be rightly understood by people in our time. Spiritual science has been given to them for this purpose, in that it brings them a deep understanding of the mysteries of the etheric Christ and a knowledge—arising out of these mysteries—of the forces of evil.

In the following words, Rudolf Steiner speaks about the direct relationship which exists between the mystery of death and the mystery of evil in our fifth post-Atlantean epoch, or, to be more precise, from the twentieth century onwards:

> Today when Christ is to appear again—though now in etheric form—when a kind of Mystery of Golgotha is to be experienced anew, evil will have a significance similar to that which birth and death had for the fourth post-Atlantean epoch ... Thus by a strange paradox mankind will in the fifth post-Atlantean epoch be led through the forces of evil to the renewal of the Mystery of Golgotha. Through

> the experience of evil it will be possible for the Christ to appear again, just as He appeared in the fourth post-Atlantean epoch through the experience of death.[3]

From this it follows that the main distinctive quality of our time is precisely the fact that both streams of forces—those of death and evil—have for the first time intersected and begun to work simultaneously, whereas in the previous, fourth epoch the former predominated, and in the next, sixth epoch the latter will predominate. For this reason, when Rudolf Steiner was asked in a private conversation about his principal task in this incarnation, he answered with two words: 'Reincarnation and karma'.* For the renewal of these ancient teachings out of the sources of esoteric Christianity in the epoch of the consciousness soul is directly connected with penetrating into the mysteries of death and evil. Furthermore, it is altogether impossible to approach these two central mysteries of earthly evolution without at the same time entering into the essential nature of the laws of reincarnation and karma. Thus only through a knowledge of the mystery of death is man able today to arrive at a full development of the consciousness soul—and through a knowledge of the mystery of evil truly to direct it to the new spirituality. Rudolf Steiner speaks of this as follows: 'The task of the forces which bring death to human beings is to give man the full capacity to develop the consciousness soul', whereas the forces of evil 'exist

---

* In a conversation with W.J. Stein in April 1922 in The Hague.

precisely in order that man might at the stage of the consciousness soul break through to the life of the spirit'.[4]

This 'full capacity to develop the consciousness soul' consists above all in the awakening within it of the forces of the individual ego, which can only happen if this ego is aware of itself as a citizen of that supersensible world through which it passes every time between death and a new birth. In another context Rudolf Steiner characterises this process as the transformation of the consciousness soul into the 'imaginative soul' on the path of spirit-pupilship.[5] But it is completely impossible for the consciousness soul to receive the new 'spiritual life' (that is, its spiritualisation in the direction of the Spirit-Self) without a conscious insight into the way in which the laws of karma work in the world, inasmuch as the highest spirituality accessible to an earthly human being is associated with it. After all, according to spiritual science all nine divine-spiritual hierarchies—from the Angels to the Seraphim—take part in its forming.[6]

Only on the basis of the new, spiritual-scientific understanding of the idea of reincarnation, therefore, is it possible to enter into the mystery of death, that is, into the mystery of how, by passing from incarnation to incarnation, a human being is able ever more and more to receive into himself the forces of the Resurrection which have entered into earthly evolution through the Mystery of Golgotha, in order ultimately—at the end of earthly time—truly to overcome death through the power of the living Christ.

Similarly, only by gaining insight into the way in which the laws of karma work in the world, in the new, Christian understanding of them as presented in Anthroposophy, can we be enabled to grasp the mystery of evil and its transformation into good, which is possible through the fact that, simultaneously with His etheric appearance to humanity, the Christ is gradually becoming the Lord of Karma for the whole of earthly evolution.[7] This is also the source of that connection between His Second Coming and the mystery of evil which has been mentioned above.

★

The aim of what follows will be to look more closely at the working of evil in the world and also at ways of opposing it, inasmuch as all this is connected with the central mystery of our time—the appearance of Christ in an etheric form.

The appropriateness of raising such a question follows above all from the deeply significant fact that the year 1998 represented a third appearance in the historical development of mankind of the apocalyptic number 666. Each of these recurrences signifies a considerable intensification of the forces of evil in earthly evolution. Such a strengthening of the forces of evil is taking place in our time, and it will, without doubt, continue in the immediate future. However, in order truly to understand the essential nature of what is taking place, it is necessary not only to turn to the two previous periods when this number was exerting an influence amongst mankind but also to explain what real occult powers and beings stand behind it. Here spiritual science can come to our aid.

According to Rudolf Steiner's spiritual-scientific research, in the process of the cosmic evolution of our Earth—which forms the fourth aeon of world evolution—it was preceded by three other aeons. However, only in the Earth aeon has man reached the stage of the individual ego, while in the previous aeons he existed only in forms similar to modern animals, plants and minerals. Thus in the very first aeon of 'Old Saturn' the future human being had only a physical body (of warmth), while his consciousness at that time resembled that of modern minerals. On 'Old Sun' he was endowed with an etheric body and through this rose to the level of plant existence. On 'Old Moon' he was provided with an astral body, as a result of which he became similar to an animal; and only on the Earth, when he received an individual ego, did he become man.

While the future human being was thus passing in the previous aeons of world evolution through the stages of mineral, plant and animal, other—higher—beings had at that time already reached their 'human' stage. The beings passing through their human stage in the aeon of Old Moon have become Angels in the Earth aeon, that is, pure spirits who have risen one hierarchic stage above man. The beings passing through their human stage on Old Sun had reached the rank of Angels in the aeon of Old Moon, and have risen in the Earth aeon to the still higher rank of Archangels. These are beings who now stand two hierarchic stages higher than man. Finally, the beings who reached their human stage on Old Saturn have by the time of the Earth aeon risen three stages higher than man, and in Christian esotericism they are called Archai.

However, not all the beings concerned have been fully able to reach their goal in the manner described. Some of them have fallen behind, and in their attempt to make up in the next aeon—under altogether different and unsuitable circumstances—for what they have omitted to do have inevitably become spirits of hindrance, who are forever overstepping the bounds of their rightful activity and, hence, making the beings passing in each aeon through their rightful development disposed towards evil. For they can no longer make up for what they have neglected in their own realm, and they therefore try to achieve it parasitically at the expense of other beings.

In this sense, spiritual science speaks of three kinds of opposing spirits, who fell behind, respectively, in the aeons of Saturn, Sun and Moon. These beings, or 'fallen spirits', it calls—in accordance with the names of their leaders—the Luciferic, Ahrimanic and Asuric beings of evil. The first of these are the Angels who fell behind on Old Moon, the second are the Archangels who fell behind on Old Sun, and the third are the Archai who fell behind on Old Saturn.[8] And as man received, respectively, his astral, etheric and physical bodies in the course of these three aeons, it is also mainly towards these that the temptations proceeding from these demonic beings are directed. Thus the Luciferic beings make a particular endeavour to penetrate man's astral body, which represents for them the most favourable opportunities for their own development; for the astral body was given to man in the period of Old Moon, that is, in that aeon when these spirits themselves became retarded in their evolution. Similarly, the Ahrimanic beings endeavour to master the forces of the human etheric body, in order with their help to make up for what they have lost; and the Asuric beings from our time onwards are increasingly approaching man's physical body (in its supersensible aspects).

Man is conscious of his encounters with the temptations of these three categories of opposing beings in his soul, which—according to spiritual science—consists of three soul members: the sentient soul, the intellectual soul and the consciousness soul. The first of these is the bearer of all the fruits of the work of the human ego on the astral body, the second bears within itself the fruits of its work on the etheric body, and the third on the physical body. From this there also follows the particular affinity of the opposing spirits with these soul members: the temptations of Lucifer appear with particular intensity in the sentient soul, those of Ahriman in the intellectual soul and of the Asuras in the consciousness soul. And as it is in the latter that the activity of the individual ego is fully manifesting itself for the first time in man, it follows that the Asuric spirits are especially dangerous for its development. For this reason Rudolf Steiner characterises them as the destroyers of the human ego itself.[9]

Likewise in the general evolution of mankind, these three categories of retarded spirits do not intervene simultaneously but only in accordance with the evolution of man himself. The first to intervene in earthly evolution was Lucifer. As the spirit of temptation, he approached man in the epoch of ancient Lemuria, an event which is described in the Bible as the 'Fall'. Ahriman with his hosts entered human evolution later, in the epoch of ancient Atlantis, while the Asuric spirits are beginning to intervene only in the epoch of the consciousness soul or, to be more precise, from our time onwards. As we shall see, the history of the twentieth century is indeed a terrifying witness of this.

To sum up what has been said: whereas a rightful evolution is expressed in occult language by the number 7, which is the number of perfection and is at the same time an expression of the fundamental law of world evolution, any development which does not reach its goal must be designated by the number 6, or the number of imperfection, the number of division and opposition (3 and 3). For this reason, each of the three categories of opposing spirits characterised above can—by virtue of their having fallen behind their rightful evolution—be designated by the number 6. As a result we obtain three sixes, which make up that apocalyptic number referred to by John in the Book of Revelation as the 'number of the Beast', which is also a 'human number'. (Rev.13:18)

However, this is not all there is to the mystery of evil. Indeed, behind the number of the Apocalypse is hidden the mystery of a mightier demonic being, who makes use of all three categories of opposing beings for the purpose of his intervention in earthly evolution. For in contrast to them, this being does not belong to this evolution. All evolution that is connected with man has passed through the three aeons of Saturn, Sun and Moon, and so all the beings who have become retarded in their development during these three periods nevertheless belong to it. They are the spirits of hindrance engendered by this very evolution. It is quite a different matter with the Beast from the abyss, behind the figure of which is concealed a mighty demonic being who does not belong to human evolution and has fallen from his rightful course of evolution in world epochs prior to ancient Saturn.

Making use of the correspondence between figures and letters in the ancient Hebrew alphabet, Rudolf Steiner reveals the significance in letters of the apocalyptic number, thus arriving at the name of the Beast: Sorat.[10] In world evolution he is the 'Sun demon'—the chief antagonist of the Christ in our cosmos. Whereas the Christ is the highest God of the human ego, its heavenly archetype and goal, Sorat appears in the cosmos as the opponent of any ego, not merely the human ego but of the principle of the ego as such, wherever it may be manifested.

As he does not have any possibility of himself entering

into the evolution of earthly humanity (his direct intervention will take place only in the apocalyptic future), Sorat tries to influence it mainly through all the three categories of opposing spirits who serve him and who directly belong to him; and his influence in earthly evolution grows in accordance with the part they play in it. Thus at the period when only Luciferic beings were active in earthly evolution, his influence upon it was minimal. With the intervention of the Ahrimanic spirits on ancient Atlantis, the spirits who instructed the humanity of that time in black magic, the power of Sorat grew significantly. But from our time onwards, when the influence of the Asuric beings is also beginning to manifest itself, Sorat's power can gradually reach its apogee.* We now find ourselves at the beginning of such an epoch where there is a significant increase in the influence of Sorat upon earthly evolution. Its arrival has been marked by the return of the apocalyptic number—in the rhythm

* The word 'apogee' here should not be understood in an absolute sense but only as applied to the present period of earthly evolution, that is, in the aspect of the so-called 'little Apocalypse'. In the aspect of the 'great Apocalypse' of which John is speaking in the Book of Revelation, the culmination of the forces of Sorat in earthly evolution and their final vanquishing will come only in the very far future. Nevertheless, according to the spiritual law of reflection these future events can also appear prophetically in earlier epochs. Thus if this reservation is taken into account, many images from the Revelation of John can also be used in order to understand our own age.

of history, for the third time since the Mystery of Golgotha—in 1998.

★

In order to understand the full significance of that year, we need first to turn to the two previous manifestations of the number referred to in earthly history, when there were only Luciferic and especially Ahrimanic spirits at Sorat's disposal.* Spiritual science has the following to say about this.

In the seventh century of the Christian era, as a result of the closing by the Byzantine emperor Justinian (sixth century) of most of the philosophical schools that remained by that time where the wisdom of antiquity was still preserved, their teachers were forced to flee to Asia Minor, where their knowledge was brought together in the so-called Academy of Gondhishapur. Historians in general know very little about this academy, and so its true significance can become understandable only in the light of spiritual-scientific research. For at that time, those Ahrimanic and Luciferic beings who were under the direct influence of Sorat in the spiritual world succeeded in gaining control of all the ancient wisdom

---

* Thus Rudolf Steiner calls Sorat, on the one hand, a 'being of Ahrimanic nature' (GA 184, 11 October 1918) and, on the other, mentions Lucifer and Ahriman in connection with his activity, and also speaks about an 'Ahrimanic intervention' (GA 184, 12 October 1918).

gathered together in this academy. As a result, this being attempted by means of the Academy of Gondhishapur to introduce a very strong consciousness-soul impulse prematurely, the right epoch for which was to have begun only in the fifteenth century. If this had succeeded, the whole of earthly civilisation would have been wholly ahrimanised, and all further evolution would have been impossible. This is just what Sorat was wanting to achieve: severing man from all subsequent evolution of the Spirit-Self, Life-Spirit and Spirit-Man, with the help of an ahrimanised consciousness soul.[11]

However, this first intervention of the influences of the Sun demon in earthly evolution was decisively paralysed by the forces flowing into it at the Turning Point of Time through the Mystery of Golgotha. Another factor which, through the wisdom of the world Rulership, also helped to destroy the power of the Sun demon was the appearance of Islam on the historical scene; for its Luciferic thrust succeeded in finally drawing the Ahrimanic sting of Gondhishapur. Nevertheless, even the little which filtered into Europe through the Arab world was enough to give a one-sidedly materialistic direction to the entire subsequent development of science. Thus the sting of the first assault of Sorat on mankind has continued to have an effect upon earthly civilisation through to our own time.

The second phase of Sorat's influence on earthly evolution was manifested around 1332 in connection with the first recurrence of the apocalyptic number. At that time, the Order of the Templars was destroyed in Europe under Sorat's influence. This Order had the task of establishing a new social order in the world, with Christ at the centre of it. For the purpose of this aim, the members of the Order endeavoured to utilise the spiritual power of gold, which was to have been purified from all egoism and placed at the service of Christian evolution. Thus although the Order itself soon became remarkably rich, its individual knights were poor, and they devoted their whole lives to following the high ideals of Christianity.

The French King Philip IV, named the Fair, and the Roman Pope Clement V rose in opposition against the growing political and economic influence of the Order and also against its spiritual and moral authority, which it exercised both in Europe and beyond its bounds. The former tried to gain control of the riches of the Order, so as to use them for attaining unlimited power in Europe, while the latter wanted to undermine its spiritual and moral authority, which he saw as a danger to the sovereignty of the Church. As a result of the fabricated accusations and terrible tortures to which the Inquisition subjected hundreds of the knights, the executioners managed to extract false confessions from them which then served as a formal reason to destroy the Order. Thus with the help of Philip and Clement, possessed as they were by Ahrimanic and Luciferic spirits, Sorat succeeded at that time in ruining one of the most significant attempts at bringing about the social reconstruction of Europe in the spirit of the Christ impulse.[12]

★

In the present phase of the historical development of mankind we are experiencing the third manifestation of the apocalyptic number and, associated with it, a new intervention of the Sorat forces in earthly evolution. The characteristic feature of this period is the full manifestation of his demonic power, inasmuch as the Asuric spirits are now also at his disposal. As a result, evil is beginning to take on a completely different character, one that is distinguishable from all those forms which were characteristic of it in the past. What does this signify? To understand this more clearly, we must now turn to a consideration of the principal streams of evil in the twentieth century from the standpoint of spiritual science.

Rudolf Steiner speaks about three kinds of evil initiations which exist today at the heart of modern civilisation. These are the initiations practised in the secret societies of the English-speaking West, in the Jesuit Order and in Bolshevism:

> Those whom I have often referred to as the people at the centre of the Anglo-American world movement have initiation consciousness, even if in a way that is thoroughly disadvantageous for humanity. Everything to do with Jesuitism has initiation consciousness. And Leninism, too, has initiation knowledge of a particular kind.[13]

These three streams of evil have been joined somewhat later in the twentieth century by a fourth. This stream is based on the principle of extreme nationalism, which in our time has begun to be one of the most powerful anti-Christian impulses in modern civilisation.* For among the most important tasks of our fifth post-Atlantean epoch is the principle of overcoming—through the Christ impulse—all forms of nationalism, which must everywhere yield to a new culture based upon the principle of the individual human 'I', that is, upon a purely human principle. Rudolf Steiner speaks about this as follows: 'Christ has an important deed to carry out in the fifth ... and also the sixth post-Atlantean period: to become a helper for the Earth in finally overcoming what derives from the principle of nationalism.'[14]

In the twentieth century this deeply anti-Christian principle lay at the foundation of the Nazi movement. Hence in the following words of Rudolf Steiner one need only replace the word 'nationalism' by the word 'Nazism' in order to arrive at a clear characterisation of the two most anti-Christian movements of our century:

> These two things have arisen in opposition to all the Christian elements of the nineteenth and twentieth cen-

---

* In the present context, nationalism must be distinguished from patriotism and a genuine love for one's fatherland, in which is manifested a person's inner connection with the spirit of his people, that is, with the Archangelic being who guides it.

> turies: nationalism, the Luciferic form of anti-Christianity, and what reaches its peak in Leninism and Trotskyism, the Ahrimanic form of anti-Christianity. These are the two spades with which the grave of Christianity is to be dug. And wherever the cults of nationalism and Trotskyism are celebrated, . . . the grave is being dug for Christianity; and for one who has the insight a mood can be discerned there which is indeed that of Easter Saturday. The Bearer of Christianity rests in the grave, and people are laying a stone upon it. They are laying two stones upon the Representative of Christianity: nationalism and the false form of socialism.[15]

What above all unites both these movements is their irreconcilable hostility towards everything proceeding from the true Spirit. 'Hatred for the Spirit', says Rudolf Steiner, 'comes towards us both from nationalism and from the false form of socialism [Bolshevism]'.*[16] Hence Anthroposophy was constantly persecuted under both the Bolshevik and Nazi regimes. After the closure of anthroposophical societies by the Bolsheviks in 1923 and by the Nazis in 1935, many of their members were subjected to cruel persecutions, which were accompanied by the confiscation of their belongings, the general closure of anthroposophical institutions and sometimes even by physical extermination.

---

* Rudolf Steiner contrasts Bolshevism (Leninism), as the 'false form of socialism', with a *spiritual* socialism, whose foundation is a free spiritual life (see GA 185, 3 November 1918 and GA 186, 7 December 1918). The source of such a 'true socialism' goes back to the early Christian communities founded by the Apostles.

If one compares these four streams of evil,[17] one can discern some degree of occult connection, on the one hand between Jesuitism and National Socialism and, on the other, between certain aims of the Western lodges and the Bolshevik experiment in Eastern Europe. Thus in the Jesuit process of initiation, as it is classically represented in the so-called 'spiritual exercises' of the founder of the Order, Ignatius Loyola, we see the aspiration—deriving from certain circles of the Roman Catholic Church—to replace the Christ in earthly evolution by a quite different spiritual being whom, however, Jesuits call by the same name.[18] By nature this being is of a purely Luciferic kind, inasmuch as he wants evolution to return to the past by forcing man to subject himself fully to outward authority of a church, the Pope, some dogma or other that is being proclaimed or simply the opinion of a group or party. However, behind this longing to establish outward authority on Earth is concealed an intense struggle to achieve spiritual rulership over the world, such as Dostoyevsky has depicted in his famous 'Legend of the Grand Inquisitor'.*

There is a whole literature about the relationship of the Roman Catholic Church with the Nazi Regime. It is

---

* In the present context, as in Dostoyevsky's legend, it is *not the whole of* the Roman Catholic Church that is being spoken of but only that part of it which has succumbed to the influence of Jesuitism. (See further about this problem in S.O. Prokofieff, *The Case of Valentin Tomberg. Anthroposophy or Jesuitism?*, Temple Lodge Publishing 1997.)

sufficient here merely to recall the concordat which Hitler concluded with the Vatican in 1933, and the political support which he received at the decisive moment of his struggle for power from the Catholic Party of Germany (the so-called party of the 'Centre'), with whose help he was able to come to power, and much besides.[19] In the present context, however, some facts of a different kind are of greater importance. Thus, for example, the anti-Semitic forgery written by the Jesuits and inflicted by them in 1912 upon Russia, a document which became famous under the name 'Protocols of the Learned Elders of Zion',[20] was later adopted by the Nazi regime in Germany and became the foundation of its ideology of total annihilation of the Jews. Or the special interest which Himmler manifested in the Order of Jesuits and their 'spiritual exercises', especially at the time when the Nazis were founding their own 'Order' within the SS. It is therefore not fortuitous that the structure and methods of work of the latter are so reminiscent of the organisational principles and certain practices of the Society of Jesus.

The relationship between the leading financial circles of the English-speaking West and the coming to power in Russia of the Bolshevik junta is also no secret. The existence of the beautifully organised help which was given by these circles to Lenin and Trotsky for establishing a Bolshevik regime in Russia is today both well known and clearly documented. However, only through spiritual science are we able to penetrate more deeply into this relationship. It is evident through spiritual science that already by the end of the nineteenth century certain occult circles of the English-speaking West had worked out and carefully planned that 'socialist experiment' which, with the help of the financial structures dependent upon their authority, was successfully implemented in Russia from October 1917 onwards.[21]

As regards the nature of the initiation practised in the secret societies of the West standing behind the Russian tragedy, Rudolf Steiner indicates that the neophytes in these societies are—through the use of certain rituals of ceremonial magic—consistently inspired with the thought that the Christ is by no means a being of great stature in the spiritual world. Since their aim is to gain complete sovereignty over the world, they must therefore necessarily turn for help to another, allegedly far mightier spirit, who is actually a being of a purely Ahrimanic nature. As a reward for renouncing the Christ, the Ahrimanic spirit inspiring the members of these lodges entices them with the illusion of a so-called 'Ahrimanic immortality' which is the complete opposite of the true immortality of which Christianity speaks.[22] The future for which these secret societies of the West are gradually preparing earthly humanity was prophetically indicated by Vladimir Solovyov in his *A Short Story of Antichrist*. For it is they who, equipped as they are with the world capital which serves them and with the help of a total globalisation, are proving themselves to be the mightiest and most active helpers of Ahriman at the time of his incarnation on Earth at the beginning of the next millennium.* And since Ahriman will incarnate 'in the West', and will, moreover, be English-speaking,† it follows from this that the English-speaking peoples will have to endure the greatest temptations in connection with his appearance. Hence a real knowledge about the secret societies of the West and their occultly political aims—of which one can learn something today only through spiritual science—is of particular importance for the Western peoples themselves, if they want to fulfil their true task in the evolution of mankind.

From everything that has been said it becomes understandable why, on the plane of outward history, these secret societies of the West are so active in their opposition to the Jesuits and vice versa. For in the one case 'experiments' are being undertaken in which the future is being anticipated in an Ahrimanic way. What in

* These secret societies of the West and their occultly political aims must be strictly distinguished from the true tasks of the Western peoples and their high culture. For these secret societies are really the greatest enemies of these peoples and of their true destiny in earthly evolution.

† GA 195, 28 December 1919. That Ahriman will incarnate in the *English-speaking* West is borne out by a surprising remark by Rudolf Steiner (ibid) to the effect that his earthly name could be, for example, 'John William Smith'. In this connection, there is much to be said for the idea that this incarnation will take place in North America, inasmuch as certain features of its occult geography (the relationship with the forces of the Ahrimanic double) will be extremely favourable to this (cf. GA 178, 16 November 1917).

the sixth cultural epoch must needs come about as a spiritual uniting of humanity is being replaced in the fifth epoch by its materialistic caricature, which is not only leading to tragedy in the present but is also shutting out practically all possibilities of future human evolution. And this is what the Western lodges are aiming at in order to consolidate their power over the world. The Jesuits, in contrast, are—as a result of their occult training—trying to turn the spiritual evolution of humanity back to the past, by subjecting man to the outer authority of the Church, the Pope, various encyclicals and regulations, as was appropriate only in the fourth cultural epoch.*

From an occult point of view, both the Jesuits and the Western lodges are above all combatting the free and conscious development of the human ego. The former try to bind humanity to forms of spiritual life which were appropriate only before the consciousness soul epoch (the Jesuit Government in Paraguay is a very clear example of this), whereas the latter want to paralyse all development of the forces of the individual ego by means of a total materialisation of the consciousness soul, as is now taking place everywhere in modern Western civilisation.

The occult relationship which has been established between the political manoeuvrings of the Western secret societies and the emergence in Eastern Europe of the Bolshevik dictatorship, on the one hand, and also

---

* In the twentieth century organisations such as 'Opus Dei' serve a similar aim within the Roman Catholic Church.

between the impulse of Jesuitism and the occult foundations of National Socialism, on the other, also enables us to understand the essential difference between them, consisting as it does above all of a colossal progression on the part of the forces of evil. For the evil forces manifesting in the twentieth century in Bolshevism have a qualitatively different character from all the forms of evil arising out of the occult aspirations of the Western secret societies. Similarly, we have an extraordinary growth in the forces of evil—not only quantitatively but also qualitatively—in the transition from Jesuitism to Nazism.

We are touching here upon a mystery in human evolution which only spiritual science is capable of revealing. It has to do with the twofold origin of evil in earthly evolution. We already touched upon this mystery at the beginning of the present essay by indicating that there exist evil forces whose sources are to be sought within earthly evolution itself—which also includes the three previous cosmic aeons of Saturn, Sun and Moon—and the forces of evil not originally deriving from it. Retarded beings such as Lucifer, Ahriman and Asur, together with their hosts, belong to the first kind of forces, while Sorat, the Sun demon, is of the second kind.

In this sense Rudolf Steiner also characterises the principal difference between the occult streams in question: 'There are three streams of initiation involved here: two of them lie on the plane of human evolution [the Western lodges and the Jesuits] and then there is one with vast, almost immeasurably vast, strength of will forces which lies beneath it [Bolshevism]'.[23] And then, in the same lecture, Rudolf Steiner defines this Bolshevik initiation as follows: 'It is an Ahrimanic initiation which simply belongs to another world sphere from our own. But it is an initiation which has within it the power to destroy everything on Earth that has arisen by way of human civilisation.' As a result of this particular demonic initiation,* all the main founders of Bolshevism become the direct tools of Ahrimanic spirits: 'Lenin, Trotsky and others similar to them are the instruments of these Ahrimanic powers'.

However, the Ahrimanic beings by whom the founders of Bolshevism were possessed do not in the context in question represent the ultimate degree of the evil working through them. For in this case, as regards its occult nature, Bolshevism would belong to earthly evolution. But Rudolf Steiner explicitly indicates that it originates from a completely different world sphere, one that has nothing in common with ours. In the lecture referred to he merely hinted at those infernal forces which ultimately lie at the foundation of Bolshevism and which simply avail themselves of Ahrimanic spirits within the earthly sphere for the fulfilment of their destructive aims: 'In Leninism the cleverness of the human animal, of the human animal nature, works its way to the surface of human evolution.' At this point one can hardly help

* See further about the Bolshevik initiation in the work cited in Note 17.

calling to mind the words from the Revelation of John: 'Here is wisdom. Let him who has understanding reckon the number of the Beast, for it is a human number'. (ch.13:18)

Rudolf Steiner fully revealed the occult mystery of Bolshevism only at the very end of his life. In the cycle of lectures which he gave in September 1924 for the priests of the Christian Community and which consisted of a spiritual-scientific study of the Apocalypse, he said: 'The modern condition of Russia—this is what the demons of Sorat who are invading human souls are striving towards'.[24]

Thus the principal occult difference between the Western lodges and Bolshevism is that the former are inspired only by demonic spirits belonging to our evolution, whereas the latter receives its inspirations from the infernal spheres below it. A similar conclusion can also be drawn by comparing Jesuitism with National Socialism. Here too, if one turns from the one stream to the other, one is aware of a colossal strengthening of evil forces. The reason for this is the fact that, like Bolshevism, Nazism in its deep, occult core is inspired by evil forces which originate not from human but from sub-human evolution. Rudolf Steiner refers to this in a slightly veiled form in the words already quoted above, where he juxtaposes Leninism (Bolshevism) and nationalism—which reached its culmination in the twentieth century in National Socialism—as the two main anti-Christian movements of our time.

However, the mystery of the occult roots of this demonic movement, which came to power in Germany in 1933, was fully revealed by Rudolf Steiner in that same lecture-cycle for the priests. There we read: 'But before the etheric Christ will be able to be rightly understood, mankind will have to cope with the beast who will rise up [from the abyss] in 1933'.[25] Thus with the coming to power in Germany of the party of Hitler, the second channel for the intervention of the Sun demon in earthly evolution opened up. The first channel, as we have seen, was Bolshevism, which seized power in Russia in 1917.* It follows from this that, just as Bolshevism represents the greatest opposition to the true tasks of Russia, National Socialism likewise represents the greatest opposition to the true tasks of Germany and German culture in the evolution of mankind.

And so in the twentieth century we have two instances of Sorat's intervention in the historical development of mankind prior to 1998, that is, prior to the third recurrence of the number of the Beast in earthly evolution. How can this phenomenon be explained from the standpoint of spiritual science? To achieve this it is necessary to turn to an important law governing evolution as a whole about which Rudolf Steiner has written on more than one occasion in his books.[26] This law states

---

* Hence we should not be surprised that these two Sorat streams are at present trying to unite in Russia, where they are giving rise to various National-Bolshevik and Communo-Fascist parties and political groups.

that every time evolution is about to rise to a new level, the previous stages are first recapitulated in a metamorphosed form. Thus at the dawn of the Earth aeon there first took place a brief repetition of the main cosmic stages which preceded it: Old Saturn, Old Sun, Old Moon; and only after this did the actual 'earthly' evolution begin.

This law works not only in the sense of positive evolution but also in the strengthening of evil forces. For evil is not in itself a creative principle in the universe, and so it always tries to make use of an already existing one to achieve its aims, distorting and demonising it. And so the third manifestation on the historical plane of the number of the beast in 1998 is preceded by a recapitulation, albeit in a different form, of the two previous periods, when under its sign the Academy of Gondhishapur came into being and the Templar Order was destroyed.

Here a quite distinctive historical perspective opens up before us, one that connects the occult foundations of Bolshevism with the impulse of Gondhishapur in the seventh century, and National Socialism with the impulse of Philip IV and Clement V in the fourteenth century.

The origin of the occult roots of Bolshevism in the demonic impulse of Gondhishapur was fully discussed in another book by the present author.* Here we shall make no more than a very brief reference to this. If we turn to the general situation in spiritual history as

---

* See Note 17.

pertained in the seventh Christian century, it can be characterised as follows. At that time the overwhelming majority of the inhabitants of Europe were on the level of development of the sentient soul. Being able neither to read nor to write, they were virtually untouched by civilisation as it was then. This civilisation consisted only of a numerically very small section of so-called educated people, amongst whom the chief means of social intercourse had increasingly become the Latin language. These people were at that time at the level of development of the intellectual soul. Amidst such a constellation in spiritual history, the demonised consciousness soul impulse issuing from the Academy of Gondhishapur must have worked like a death-bringing venom, capable of poisoning the souls of Europeans to the point where they would be deprived of all possibility of spiritual development in the future.

We had a similar constellation in Russia at the beginning of the twentieth century. Here, too, the large part of the population at that time was still at the stage of development of the sentient soul, and was almost wholly untouched by European civilisation in general. A comparatively small, albeit very active, educated stratum of society remained for the most part at the stage of the intellectual soul (and the Russian cultural renaissance at the beginning of the twentieth century arose from this). The consciousness soul, on the other hand, was represented only by very few of those active in Russian culture at that time. It was into this constellation of spiritual history that the Bolsheviks introduced the destructive impulse of the demonised consciousness soul. Thus in the Bolshevik Revolution of 1917 there again appeared on the scene of European history the forces of the Sun demon which had stood behind the Academy of Gondhishapur in the seventh century, this time making the attempt to tear Russia away from its task on behalf of humanity in general in the sixth cultural epoch.

We can discern a similar kind of occult relationship between the destruction of the Templar Order in the fourteenth century and the coming to power of the National Socialists in Germany in the twentieth century. Here the most important components of Nazi ideology and anti-human practice are simply a demonic distortion of those radiant and deeply Christian ideals towards which the Templars were striving.

In this connection it is particularly striking how Rudolf Steiner characterises the spiritual endeavours of the Templar knights. In the lecture of 25 September 1916[27] he indicates that the most important thing for them was the principle of blood and soil. For the Templars saw their particular task as being the conquest of the Holy Land and above all Jerusalem for the entire Christian world, as the place where the Mystery of Golgotha took place historically. However, they wanted to do this not for themselves but in order to dedicate this region to Christ. In subsequent times the whole Earth was to be consecrated to Him, for in inner circles of the Order there was a knowledge of that central mystery of esoteric Christianity, that since the Mystery of Golgotha Christ has been its new Spirit, and the Earth His new cosmic body. For this reason the Templars endeavoured to extend their influence to other territories in Europe and beyond, in order gradually to establish everywhere a new social order, at whose centre the Christ Himself would be found. The Templars derived their ideas of such a new social order from *imaginations* imbued with the Christ impulse, which they experienced in their souls as a result of the Christian initiation that they had received.

The Templars aspired towards 'imbuing all European culture with Christ'.[28] In order to achieve this goal, each of the knights had to be ready to give away even his life, that is, sacrifice every drop of his blood. For the Templars knew from their initiation that man's blood is connected with his ego, the divine archetype of which was manifested to humanity in Christ's appearance on the Earth. Thus a vow was incorporated in the initiation of the Templars whereby they consecrated their blood to Him. Rudolf Steiner describes this as follows:

> A central concern of the Templars was that everyone in the Order should know that his blood does not belong to him but that it must be dedicated to bringing [the forces of] the Mystery of Golgotha in a spiritual sense to Western and, to an extent, to Eastern humanity. And what emanated from such a sacrificial mood of the Templars with regard to the Mystery of Golgotha was gradually transformed into a kind of Christian initiation.[29]

And then in another lecture:

> In addition to the monastic vows that were customary at that time ... the Templar knights considered it their duty to make every effort to bring the places where the Mystery of Golgotha had occurred under European sovereignty. They were not to think of anything other ... than imbuing their hearts and souls with the sacred mystery of Golgotha, and also of devoting every drop of their blood to bringing the Holy Land under the sway of European authority ... Their blood was to belong not to them but solely to the task which we have indicated.[30]

Thus in the inspiration of the Templars the principle of the soil and the principle of blood played a truly central role. For in dedicating to Christ one or another earthly territory which came under their authority, they experienced it in their souls as being a chalice which they were sacrificially offering up to Christ; and in consecrating their blood to Him, they experienced it as the contents of the chalice which they were offering up together with it. As a result, the knights of the Temple were able to experience in their souls the true mystery of the Holy Grail. Hence in one of his lectures Rudolf Steiner calls the Templars the 'messengers of the Holy Grail'.*

---

* From an undated lecture of 1904, published in the journal *Gäa Sophia*, no.3, 1929. See also GA 93, 22 May 1905.

When, after the official closing of the Order by the Pope, many of its knights were subjected to terrible tortures, which were carried out with a particular refinement at the personal orders of Philip the Fair,* demons—the servants of Sorat—began to speak through their consciousness, darkened as it was by inhuman torments; and the true teaching and the real aims of the Order were thereby turned into their complete opposite. Rudolf Steiner speaks of this as follows:

> If one looks at what was going on during the tortures in those people who were being condemned as Templars, one

---

* In connection with this, Rudolf Steiner speaks about a special 'Ahrimanic initiation in gold' received by Philip, through which he was able to direct the tortures of the Templars in such a way that they led to these results. The sources of this demonic initiation are to be sought in a past incarnation of Philip, when he was one of the leading priests of the black-magic mysteries of ancient Mexico, in which human sacrifices were practised that were accompanied by monstrous tortures of the innocent victims (see the description of these mysteries in the lecture of 24 September 1916, GA 171). Rudolf Steiner refers in a veiled form to this previous incarnation of the French king in the following words: 'And so it could happen that certain knowledge entered the soul of Philip the Fair . . . which belonged to that kind of knowledge as was revealed in the cruel and repulsive Mexican mysteries . . . As if out of deeply subconscious impulses, he found the means of introducing certain impulses into human evolution by putting people to death. For this he needed victims' (GA 171 25 September 1916). A further metamorphosis of these methods can be discerned in the practices of the concentration camps and gas chambers of the Nazis.

> can receive the impression that what was living in the visions of the Templars was inspired by Sorat. As a result they slandered themselves, and it was easy to find them guilty on the basis of what came from their own lips. A terrible scene was enacted before the onlookers: those who imagined themselves to be something completely different were not able to speak about this during the tortures, and various spirits from Sorat's hosts spoke through them, uttering monstrous things against the Order from the lips of its own members.[31]

If we now turn to what was said through them by Sorat's demons (only an insignificant part of what they said has been preserved in the records of the trial), it is not difficult to discern a certain portent of Nazi ideology, with its utter loathing of Christianity and its urge to revive various demonic cults of pagan antiquity. Especially the principle of blood and soil, which played such an important part in the initiation of the Templars, was turned by the Nazis into its total opposite. What for the Templars was a path of sacrificial and selfless service of the Christ became in the Nazi ideology of 'blood and soil' a very strong anti-Christian impulse, the 'second stone' (after Bolshevism) which the Sun demon succeeded in laying on Christ's grave.

Returning now to the universal law of recapitulation mentioned above, it is possible to confirm the fact of a recapitulation of the first manifestation of the number of the Beast in the seventh century in Bolshevism and of its second manifestation in the fourteenth century in

National Socialism.* However, if one compares these streams of evil it is impossible not to see an immense difference between them, such as has already been pointed out—namely, a colossal strengthening of the power of evil manifesting in Bolshevism and National Socialism in comparison with the impulse of Gondhishapur and even with the destruction of the Templars. The reason for this from the occult point of view is that both the first and the second manifestations of the number of the Beast on the historical scene took place *before* the consciousness soul epoch (it began in 1413), which was when the Asuric spirits also became involved in human evolution for the first time. Of the latter Rudolf Steiner has the following to say: 'The Asuras will develop evil with a far greater intensity than even the

---

* In accordance with this spiritual law, the second manifestation on the scene of history of the number of the beast in the fourteenth century was preceded by a recapitulation of its first manifestation in the seventh. The event which can be regarded as such a recapitulation was the 8th Ecumenical Council in Constantinople (AD 869), when, 'under the direct influence of the impulse of Gondhishapur, the Catholic Church' officially abolished the principle of the spirit in man's being and adopted the dogma that it consists only of body and soul (GA 182, 16 October 1918). Another such recapitulation was the work of the Franciscan monk Roger Bacon in the thirteenth century, who taught under the influence of the impulse of Gondhishapur (GA 184, 12 October 1918), and also the stream of Nominalism, which arose in Europe out of the same source and did much to contribute towards science taking its modern *materialistic* form.

Satanic [Ahrimanic] powers in the age of Atlantis or than the Luciferic spirits in Lemuria'.[32] Thus whereas in the seventh and fourteenth centuries only Luciferic and Ahrimanic spirits were at Sorat's disposal in earthly evolution, in the consciousness soul epoch Asur with his hosts also joined them, with the result that there was that extreme strengthening of evil that we witness in Bolshevism and National Socialism. For only now that all three categories of opposing spirits have become included in earthly evolution has the number of the Beast reached its culmination, and Sorat himself has for the first time been able to manifest the entire fullness of his infernal powers.

Thus in the monstrous crimes of Bolshevism and Nazism, with their extermination camps, total terror, gas-chambers of death, the genocide of entire peoples and so on, we have for the first time in earthly history the manifestation of the combined activity of *all three* categories of opposing forces serving the chief opponent of the Christ in our cosmos—the Sun demon, Sorat. However, the leading part in their combined activity will gradually pass to the Asuric spirits, of whom from our time onwards Sorat will increasingly make use in his battle with the human ego.

★

As we turn to the third appearance of the number of the Beast on the arena of history, we must not limit the sphere of activity of this demonic impulse to 1998 alone.

This date merely signifies a certain occult-historical landmark on the path whereby evil has entered earthly evolution, in a manner similar to its first and second appearance. For neither the flowering of the Academy of Gondhishapur nor the destruction of the Order of the Templars precisely coincided with the corresponding years which reflect the rhythm of the apocalyptic number.

With this reservation, we can now approach an investigation of certain basic symptoms of earthly civilisation at the end of our century. What strikes one most of all is the attack—hitherto unprecedented in its dimensions, pressure and refinement—upon the individual human ego. This is brought about initially through the successive destruction of its sheaths. Man's physical body is being destroyed by drugs; his etheric body by a complete sexual freedom, extending beyond the norm of the wildest perversions; while in the astral body inclinations are being consistently implanted for all kinds of violence, especially through advertisements, cinema and television. All this has the aim of weakening the individual ego to such an extent that it can without difficulty be subordinated to the demonic powers that are alien to it, and ultimately be replaced by a demonic being of a subhuman nature.

On the other hand, everything possible is being done to destroy any real connection of the human ego with the spiritual world, inasmuch as it is in the ego where a meeting of the individual with the etheric Christ can take place today. For this purpose, on the one hand, all possible kinds of atavistic—and, increasingly, overtly demonic—occultism are being disseminated amongst mankind, and, on the other, everything possible is being done to eradicate all shoots of the new supersensible faculties which lead to a conscious experience of the etheric Christ. Thus faculties for Imagination are consistently being eradicated from childhood by television, cinema, advertising, computer and 'virtual-reality' games; faculties for Inspiration are being deadened by rock music; and faculties for Intuition by a total permissiveness in the sexual realm, including the universal availability of pornography. Through all this, and also much besides, the human ego is as it were artificially 'pressed down' into the physical body and is gradually identified with it, not simply on the level of 'ideology', as is the case with ordinary materialism, but on the plane of the subconscious forces of the will.* Consequently, the human ego is taken hold of by purely animal-like, subhuman forces which know nothing of morality, conscience or compassion, and are capable of virtually anything.

What is being expressed here from an occult aspect is the influence of Asuric forces, the main opponents of the

* Many modern aspects of sport also strongly further this aim. The symptoms are everywhere available. They are expressed in moments of total mass violence and senseless aggression, and are increasingly in evidence at big sporting events.

human ego within earthly evolution. Rudolf Steiner characterises their destructive activity as follows:

> These Asuric spirits will bring it about that everything which they take hold of—and this will be man's innermost being, his consciousness soul together with his ego—will unite with earthly materiality. This will be wrested piece by piece [by the Asuras] from the ego; and to the extent that the Asuric spirits become established in the consciousness soul, man will have to leave part of his being on the Earth. What has succumbed to the Asuras will then be irretrievably lost [to man].

And he goes on:

> These Asuric forces will manifest themselves in our epoch in accordance with the spirit which reigns in it, and which we can call a spirit that comes to expression in a life where everything is subordinated to the material world alone and also in utter obliviousness of the reality of spiritual beings and spiritual worlds.[33]

As a result, man is not merely assured of his descent from the animals, as was the case under the influence of the Ahrimanic spirits who inspired the 'scientific' materialism of the nineteenth century, but under the influence of Asur and his hosts man 'will take this view seriously and will start to live in conformity with it'. In other words, 'people with such a conception of the world will live like animals, immersed in purely animal instincts and animal passions'.[34]

Thus Sorat is waging a battle against the human ego today from two sides, with the help of the demonic powers who serve him in earthly evolution. On the one hand, he strives to replace the human ego with a demonic being under his authority, and, on the other, to dissolve this ego in the forces of an animal-like will governable only by the instincts, in order to wrest piece after piece from it for the strengthening of his own demonic kingdom through the ego-substance which he has thus abducted. Both trends are in an occult sense none other than a metamorphosed repetition of Sorat's principal endeavours during the first two manifestations of his number amongst mankind. For through the Academy of Gondhishapur, he was already trying to chain the human ego to the purely animal-like rationality of the physical body by making use of its original connection with the consciousness soul; and by subjecting the Templars to inhuman tortures, he was endeavouring to force their egos to leave their bodies in order to make the demons serving him speak through the lips of the physical sheath temporarily abandoned by the individual concerned. Something similar, though on a completely different plane and with completely different technical possibilities, is being attempted by Sorat from the end of our century onwards. The result of this would be that the human ego would become wholly incapable of approaching the spiritual world where the Christ is dwelling today and from where He can and wants to help mankind.

However, the intentions of Sorat and the Asuric spirits who serve him in our time are concerned not only with completely severing man from the spiritual world and the human ego from its archetype, the Cosmic Ego of Christ, but also with awakening in man an intense hatred for this spiritual world and, ultimately, for the principle of the ego as such. For the rejection by man of his ego will lead to the 'second death' of which John the Divine speaks in his Book of Revelation. (ch. 20:14)[35]

Such hatred of everything that originates from the true Spirit will be particularly characteristic of those people who are possessed by Sorat. Rudolf Steiner describes them in the following words:

> By the end of this century he [Sorat] will make his presence felt by appearing in a number of people as that being by whom they are possessed. People will be seen to appear whom it will be impossible to think of as really being people ... Outwardly they will have active and powerful natures, with savage features and with a destructive fury in their emotions. In their faces it will even be possible to distinguish animal-like features. It will be possible to recognise these Sorat people outwardly because they not only mock everything connected with the Spirit in a quite appalling way but also oppose it, trying all they can to vilify it.[36]

If we look around us, we can already notice that such people are appearing with regard to whom we virtually have to ask ourselves: to what extent are they 'really people' and not demons in the flesh or wild animals in human form?[37] Above all this applies to those specific crimes which have increasingly become a mass phenomenon in the last quarter of the twentieth century. Here it is enough to mention such symptoms as terrorism and 'ethnic cleansing', and the monstrous crimes against children. In the case of the former, as a rule, what is manifested more is a savage and fanatical will governed by—often pseudo-religious or nationalistic—instincts, while with the latter the human ego has been completely taken over by a demonic being.

Here, however, the question arises: can one really call these crimes the most terrible after twentieth century humanity has already experienced the horrors of Auschwitz and Kolyma? Nevertheless, there is one essential difference here, the full significance of which will be manifested in the not so distant future. For what appeared in Bolshevism and Nazism was, so to speak, an already 'mature fruit' on the world tree of evil. Hence the roots of this evil reach deep into many centuries of human history, and its manifestation in such monstrous forms has been preceded by a long preparation and a gradual 'ripening'. In contrast, we are today for the first time coming up against completely new forms of evil which are only now entering into human evolution and are still at the very beginning of their development, an evil which derives its impulses from the abyss marked by the third appearance of the apocalyptic number.

The main difference between the modern forms of evil

and those that are already familiar to humanity from the tragic history of the twentieth century can be expressed as follows. Whereas formerly, be it under the Bolshevik or Nazi regime, it took the whole might of the vast State machine, beautifully organised propaganda, an ideology worked out in all its details and sometimes also a complete pseudo-religion to incline a person towards evil, kill his conscience and impoverish his moral feeling, in our time the most radical evil can enter directly into a person without any outward means, subject him to itself and turn him into its blind tool, into someone who has neither conscience, nor morality nor convictions. As a result an evil is entering the world which people are putting into effect no longer out of false beliefs or ideologies, and not even out of their egotism or a hunger for enrichment, enjoyment and so forth, but simply for its own sake, an evil which is both meaningless and cannot be explained by any rational or emotional principles. Such evil is impossible for the human mind to understand, it cannot be explained even by the most sophisticated theories; and it is also impossible to eradicate it by any means accessible to modern civilisation, inasmuch as its sources are rooted not in it but in the sub-human world. This is already apparent in the example of the total powerlessness of the most powerful and technically equipped governments in the face of terrorism, that is, in the face of an individual human personality possessed by demons.

The Nazi regime fell as a result of war, Bolshevism as a

consequence of its total economic bankruptcy;* whereas terrorism, as is shown by the present struggle against it, cannot be overcome by any of the means familiar to humanity today but only by those *spiritual means* which will be spoken about later. And modern terrorism is only a first foretaste of what is awaiting humanity in the very near future. Today the danger of terrorism even, for example, with mini atom-bombs the size of a small suitcase, or a box beneath some cigarettes, has for some time been no mere wild invention of modern science fiction, not to speak of the possibilities of chemical, biological and—no longer beyond the horizon—'genetic' weapons ... The only way to prevent people who are possessed by Sorat's demons from doing evil and, hence, from losing what alone makes a man *truly* man—his individual ego—is by educating the individual concerned in accordance with the *true* spirit from earliest childhood and also with the help of those methods which humanity will be able to develop in future on the basis of modern spiritual science.

In the cycle of lectures which he gave to the priests of the Christian Community on the Revelation of John, Rudolf Steiner refers in this connection to one particular place in this book where it speaks of locusts with human-

* We are not concerned here with the occult reasons for the fall of both regimes. That such deeper reasons exist is borne out by the fact that Nazism in Germany lasted for roughly twelve years, and Bolshevism in Russia for 72 years. Both numbers have a mystical significance.

like faces emerging from the smoke of the abyss, whose hosts are under the leadership of a demonic being bearing the name of Abaddon—which when translated means the 'destroyer', destroying everything around—and who attack humanity (ch.9). In the course of explaining the occult significance of this imaginative picture, Rudolf Steiner indicates that these hordes are none other than human beings who have been completely deprived of the human ego.[38] It is out of such people that Sorat will—by populating their sheaths with the spirits who serve him—create his infernal army on Earth, the army of Antichrist, thereby subjecting mankind to trials of vast magnitude, before which all the horrors of the twentieth century will pale.*

★

As has already been noticed by certain anthroposophical authors, the three successive manifestations of the number of the Apocalypse in human history are associated with the assault of Sorat, respectively, on man's thinking—the attempt to bring about its premature intellectualisation through the Academy of Gondhishapur; on his feeling—the destruction of the Templar Order out of

* Modern scientific experiments in the field of cloning and genetic engineering, only a relatively small portion of which have been made public (most of them have hitherto been kept secret), testify to the extent to which humanity has already seriously approached the possibility of the artificial 'production' of physical bodies for the incarnation of demons.

hatred and envy; and on his will—its increasing animalisation in our time.[39]

It is a familiar thought from spiritual science that through his thinking man is connected with the whole of humanity and through his feeling with a certain group, tribe or folk (which is why both noble patriotism and all the demonic forms of nationalism and racism are rooted in this realm); and that finally, in his will—where the forces of destiny (karma) are also working in deep unconsciousness—every human being conceives himself as an individuality who is shut up in his own shell, in his own unique microcosm where he always acts in isolation.

These facts enable one to understand more clearly why from the outset the influence of the Academy of Gondhishapur had a universally human character and why it also continues to affect modern civilisation even to this day, inasmuch as its moving force represents a picture of the thinking of materialistic science.* But this universally human character of the demonic impulse of Gondhishapur manifested especially strongly in Bolshevism,

---

* This *materialistically* tinged science—that is, gripped by Ahrimanic powers—must be strictly distinguished from those high spiritual sources whence it originally proceeded; for it is the earthly reflection of the highly noble yearning of the human individual for a free knowledge of the truth. Anthroposophy would seek to lead it once again—though on a modern level—to these deeply spiritual primal sources of true science, through Goetheanism and also through a concrete renewal of its various realms out of the true Spirit of the Time.

with its international ideology of the most radical rejection of everything spiritual, an ideology which was itself based upon that same materialistic science. Hence when speaking about the thinking of Bolsheviks such as Lenin, Lunacharsky and Trotsky, Rudolf Steiner particularly emphasises that it was the thinking of 'an utterly ... material brain',[40] while its reasoning was indeed the 'reasoning of the human animal, of a human animality',[41] that is, of the Beast from the abyss whose number is 'a human number'. (ch.13:18)

Similarly, the boundless longing for power of Philip IV was connected with overtly nationalistic interests: making France into the most influential state in the Europe of that time. This is what lay behind, on the one hand, the wars which he waged against the political independence of England and Flanders and, on the other, his struggle against too great an independence on the part of the Roman Catholic Church, his complete victory over which was marked by the so-called Avignon imprisonment of the Popes. Consequently, the Roman Catholic Church was for several decades totally dependent on the French crown as its vassal. As Philip sought to extend his influence further in Europe there remained the obstacle of the Templars; they were a particular danger to his plans because of their riches and political power, though to an even greater degree because of their high moral authority and spiritual strength. This is why the main aim of the demonic personality of Philip was not merely the physical extermination of the Order and the acquisition of its riches but, above all, its spiritual annihilation.

However, this nationalistic impulse of the Sun demon appeared most openly in the twentieth century, in National Socialism, at the very heart of whose racist doctrine was the idea of the division of the whole of humanity into a lower race of slaves and a higher race of masters, whose sole head was to be a German race wholly subordinated to the anti-Christian aspect of the principle of 'blood and soil'.

In comparison, from our time onwards, when the forces of Sorat are gradually beginning to penetrate the human will, the individual ego itself—and, with it, the entire future of earthly evolution—is exposed to danger. It follows from this that it is today the human ego which is at the focus of all human and world problems, and which is confronted by a choice: finally to succumb to evil, or consciously to turn to that spiritual world in which it can find its higher archetype in the 'I am' of Christ and, by finding it, become a victor in the great trial by evil.

★

Before turning to a description of the spiritual resources available to humanity for the battle with all the forces of opposition characterised above, it is necessary to dwell upon one particular aspect of the strengthening of the forces of evil in the immediate future. The matter in question is the incarnation of Ahriman himself on the

Earth which is impending. His incarnation will, of course, be on the direct line of the working of evil which is associated with the third appearance of the number of the Apocalypse.

In a series of lectures from the year 1919, Rudolf Steiner spoke at length about the incarnation of Ahriman at the very beginning of the new millennium as the most important test of the general spiritual maturity of mankind in the epoch of the consciousness soul.* In these lectures he also characterises a whole series of tendencies in modern civilisation which Ahriman will particularly try to make use of for his incarnation, in order that it might take place in the most favourable way for him, that is, so that it corresponds most fully with his own aims.[42] Four of these tendencies have a special significance for us, inasmuch as they shed light upon what has been said so far:

1. The triumph of materialistic science and the almost unlimited power in the world of economics and capital which this has called forth.
2. A one-sided absorption in the content of the Gospels, leading to an experience not of the real Christ but only His hallucination.
3. All forms of nationalism, and also an adherence to the principle of blood and soil.

---

* 'Before even [a small] part of the third millennium has run its course'—thus goes one of his formulations (GA 191, 1 November 1919). See also Note 42.

4. Political programmes and ideological slogans of any kind.

If we consider these four points, it is not difficult to discern their connection with the activity and intentions of the four streams of evil in occult history which have been spoken of. Thus the first point characterises the most important aims of the Western secret societies, which seek to make use of materialistic science, and the economic power based upon its universal 'triumph', for a secret and patently obvious battle with all forms of free and independent spiritual life. An experience of a mighty hallucination of Christ is arrived at through an approach to the Gospels based on the occult practising of the 'spiritual exercises' of Ignatius Loyola. Nationalism, which is today taking hold in the most diverse forms of large groups of the Earth's inhabitants, has in the twentieth century manifested the whole of its anti-human nature in the practical implementation of the racist doctrine of National Socialism. Finally, perhaps nothing has brought mankind more misfortune and suffering in the twentieth century than the attempts to implement on Earth the illusory political programmes and slogans of the Bolsheviks. Rudolf Steiner directly cites Lenin and his teachings as an example when he characterises this tendency.[43]

Thus it follows from the above correlation that all four streams of evil have actually been preparing the most favourable conditions in the twentieth century for the incarnation of Ahriman in the twenty-first, which is an indication of the extent to which the various forces of evil have been working in concord and with singleness of purpose in the modern world. Hence it is only possible to withstand them on the basis of a thoroughly clear knowledge of their essential nature, origin and aims, that is, by being fully armed with a concrete occult knowledge of them, which can only be acquired today from spiritual science. Such a deep understanding of what is going on is especially necessary in our time because only this can make available the sources of supersensible help which humanity needs today as never before.

In this connection, the following recollection of Ita Wegman can be cited of a conversation that she had with Rudolf Steiner, in which he indicated that 'only human beings are in a position to know the secrets of demons. And the Gods [hierarchies] are awaiting these secrets which human beings can communicate to them...' When, therefore, 'human beings offer up as a sacrifice to the Gods these secrets won from the demons, the dark deeds of these demons can be averted [by the hierarchies], and spiritual light can shine forth again where darkness had reigned'.*

It follows from this that the imminent arrival of Ahriman on the Earth will be a stern, but at the same

---

* Ita Wegman, *An die Freunde*, article of 4 October 1925. English edition: *Esoteric Studies, The Michael Impulse*, Temple Lodge Publishing, London 1993.

time a necessary, trial for the whole of contemporary humanity. For his coming will give human beings the opportunity to gain an insight into the most hidden intention of the opposing forces with respect to earthly evolution, in order then to communicate these secrets to the spiritual hierarchies. However, if humanity is to be able to accomplish this task in the epoch of the consciousness soul, when for the first time it has attained an inner maturity and complete freedom, a conscious choice will have to be made between the path which the shortly to be incarnated Ahriman will suggest to it through all the temptations that he will bring and the path of which Anthroposophy speaks today. This latter path is one which leads through a true understanding of the all-embracing cosmic mysteries of the living Christ to a real meeting with Him in the etheric sphere, thus opening up a new possibility of a conscious collaboration with Him and all the divine-spiritual hierarchies who serve Him in their battle with the unlawful 'prince of this world'.

Only in such an event will the coming of Ahriman in the flesh be rightly understood and met by humanity. Moreover, the trials associated with his coming will then merely serve to purify and further strengthen the forces of the individual ego which, through its connection with Christ, will emerge from them not only as a victor but also as the bearer of a new knowledge of the world, which—in the sense of the words of Rudolf Steiner quoted above—it will be able to communicate to the divine-spiritual hierarchies for the good of earthly evolution as a whole.

★

Before those who have already made this choice between Christ and Ahriman there now lies the task of preparing mankind for the impending arrival on the Earth of that being about whose anti-Christian nature Christ said: 'For the ruler of this world is coming; he has no power over me.' (John 14:30) This preparation will consist above all in an active spiritual opposition to those four streams of evil delineated above. And inasmuch as, in them, we are concerned with a particular kind of demonic *initiation*, it is possible to overcome them only on the basis of real occult knowledge and by consciously opposing them with spiritual work that springs from modern Christian initiation. Hence Rudolf Steiner concludes his characterisation of these streams of dark initiation with the words: 'The *only* power which can bring order and a purpose worthy of humanity into this whole stream [of initiation] is what lies within true spiritual science'.[44]

In this sense, it will be possible to overcome the power of the Western lodges only through conscious and active work towards bringing a threefold social organism into being in the world, the only kind of social order which is 'in accordance with Christ'[45] and is, therefore, capable of withstanding all the anti-Christian tendencies in the social life of mankind. For the consequences of the now extant globalisation and the ravaging of a large part of humanity that is associated with it will inescapably lead to such catastrophes and social upheavals that only a threefold social order will be able to lead humanity out of the all-encompassing crisis in which it will inevitably find itself as a result of the present policies of the secret societies of the West. Rudolf Steiner said in this connection: 'The Anglo-American element may well achieve world dominion; but without threefoldness [of the social organism] this dominion will flood the world with the death and sickness of culture . . . '.[46]

The overcoming of Jesuitism—not only in religious life but also in practically all spheres of modern culture where it has penetrated during the last few centuries—will be possible only through a conscious opposition to the demonised initiation of the will lying at its foundation such as can be achieved through a true Christian-Rosicrucian initiation, which also aims to develop the principle of the will,[47] though in an opposite direction. For its foundation is the total acknowledgement of individual freedom and the absolute inviolability of the will, as the holy of holies of every human being. This Rosicrucian initiation, of which Anthroposophy is the modern representative, in contrast to Jesuitism—which tries to take all the spiritual strivings of an individual human being under its control—wants to lead him to a new, conscious and free entry into the spiritual world, in accordance with the words of Christ: 'And you will know the truth, and the truth will set you free'. (John 8:32) This is why the Jesuits have from the outset been fighting such a fierce battle against spiritual science.* For, in Rudolf Steiner's words, 'in the development of civilisation during the last few centuries, there is hardly a greater contrast than that between Jesuitism and Rosicrucianism'.[48]

Similarly, all forms of nationalism, racism and other current ways of dividing humanity in accordance with physical differences must be opposed by the Michaelic impulse working now in earthly evolution. For in our time Michael, the ruling spirit of the Age, turns to the whole of mankind and not to a certain part of it. Moreover, in the course of his ascent to the rank of Time-Spirit during the second half of the nineteenth century, Michael had to sustain a hard battle in the spiritual worlds with the Ahrimanic spirits of darkness, whom he cast down from the higher spheres to the earthly world around 1879. These spirits of darkness who have penetrated into humanity have in the twentieth century become the inspirers of all the modern kinds of nationalism.[49] Hence all forms of chauvinism, nationalism and racism in our time constitute an open battle against the Michaelic impulse, which is always directed solely to the individual ego and never to the bodily sheaths which determine an individual's affinity to one or

* Rudolf Steiner often referred in his lectures to this battle of the Jesuits with spiritual science as they conceived it, a battle whose principal resource was and remains slander and distortion of the truth; and he also cited concrete examples and quotations from Jesuit writings. See also op.cit. in footnote on page 23.

another group (astral body), a particular people (etheric body) or race (physical body). Rudolf Steiner speaks as follows about this opposition between the aspirations of Michael on the one hand and nationalism on the other:

> Among the things that would wholly reject the impulse of Michael today are all feelings of nationality. They flared up in the nineteenth century and have become stronger and stronger in the twentieth . . . All this is in direct opposition to the Michael principle; all this contains Ahrimanic forces which oppose the influence of the Michael forces upon the earthly life of man.[50]

Finally, Bolshevism—which through a tragic confluence of circumstances arose in Russia and has far from exhausted its influence there—needs to be opposed by the best and most spiritual qualities which Rudolf Steiner describes as the essential qualities of the Russian people, those deep reservoirs of energies which live within it today as precursors of the sixth cultural epoch. In this connection Rudolf Steiner characterises the Russian people as the 'Christ people', remarking that 'the Christ is ever present as an inner aura impregnating the thinking and feeling of this people'.[51] This is also the source of its predisposition for a deep understanding of Christianity, for its 'Sophian' perception. (It is not for nothing that it came to Russia under the sign of the Sophia.) Rudolf Steiner speaks in this connection of the 'unconquerable Grail mood' living in the Russian people upon which its entire future rests.[52] It is with this 'Grail mood' that the Russian people must oppose Bolshevism, in order that it may recognise and overcome its Satanic nature most especially within its own soul.

In our time the fullest revelation of the mysteries of the Holy Grail is contained in Anthroposophy, which Rudolf Steiner for this reason calls the 'science of the Grail'[53]—hence the essential predisposition of Russian people for an anthroposophical understanding of man and the world, even if they are today far from conscious of this. Deriving as it does its knowledge directly from the wisdom of the mysteries of the Holy Grail, which represent the spiritual focus of esoteric Christianity as a whole, Anthroposophy contains within itself the spiritual forces which can finally overcome the terrible sickness of Bolshevism not only in Russia but amongst the whole of mankind.

Thus through Anthroposophy we are not only able to comprehend with our clear, waking consciousness the true nature and the secret intentions of evil forces in our world but something even more important—to oppose them with the active power of goodness springing from the depths of Christian esotericism. The Western secret societies can be opposed by the impulse of the threefold social organism; the aspirations of the Jesuits by the Christian-Rosicrucian path of initiation; all forms of nationalism and racism by the impulse of Michael, the guiding spirit of our age; and the Satanic phenomenon of Bolshevism by the wisdom and moral forces streaming from the modern 'science of the Grail'. And this is, after all, one of the central tasks of humanity in the epoch of the consciousness soul: to learn from its encounters with evil to develop that greater power of goodness which connects man with the ultimate source of all powers of goodness—the supersensible domain of the etheric Christ (the true Shambala).

★

In order that this battle with evil on the plane of outward history may really be crowned with success, it is necessary to supplement it with an active opposition to the demonic beings in one's own soul. Thus overcoming the forces of Lucifer in the sentient soul depends on making a constant effort to achieve true self-knowledge and self-perfection. To the extent that every human being tries to rid himself of his lower passions, desires, pride and all amoral inclinations, he is truly conquering the Luciferic spirits in his soul. For the overcoming of Ahriman—in addition to working intensively on oneself, especially with regard to eradicating falsehood of any kind and all aspects of fear, together with all overt and secret inclinations towards materialism—something different is required, namely, a working together of human beings in the social realm that is based on spiritual principles. Establishing new social relationships out of a spiritual understanding of one another is the magic power which can conquer Ahriman in man's intellectual soul. However, in order to overcome the forces of Asur and his hosts something more is necessary—for this a human being must himself embark in freedom upon the path of modern Christian initiation of which Anthroposophy speaks. For only a strict spiritual pupilship in the sense of this path can impart to the individual human ego the inner strength capable of withstanding all the temptations of the Asuras, which are in our time only just beginning to invade humanity. Finally, opposing the power of the Sun demon himself, Sorat, is possible only through a direct relationship with the Christ Himself, as the divine 'I am' of our entire cosmos. Hence only from Him can the necessary help be found today for the battle with this cosmic adversary.

However, this relationship with Christ must in our time be attained in the consciousness soul, that is, fully consciously and freely. This is possible only through a concrete knowledge of the mysteries of the living Christ in the present, a knowledge which opens up the possibility of a direct participation in the work of Christ. Rudolf Steiner writes about this in the concluding chapter of his book *Knowledge of the Higher Worlds*.[54] In this chapter there is a description of how someone who is on the path of Christian-Rosicrucian initiation experiences the encounter with the great Guardian of the Threshold, in whom the Christ Himself appears to him.*

He approaches the human soul with the following words: 'You will some day be able to unite yourself with

* That the modern initiate is meeting the Christ Himself in the figure of the great Guardian of the Threshold is stated by Rudolf Steiner in his book *Occult Science* (GA 13).

me, but I cannot find blessedness as long as others are still unredeemed.' As he experiences this sublime moment, the Christian initiate knows that such a 'union will not be possible until all the powers which have come to the initiate from this [higher] world are applied by him to liberating and redeeming the world'. As a result, once he has been honoured with an encounter with the Christ in his personal spiritual experience the modern Christian initiate thereby becomes His conscious servant and collaborator; and he is henceforth filled with a single longing: 'to contribute to the liberation of the human race'. By virtue of this aim he now 'offers up his gifts to the altar of humanity'. He no longer belongs to himself but to all human beings. For he has fulfilled in his liberated soul the principal aim of the Christian initiate, as contained in the words: 'Not I but Christ in me'. (Gal. 2:20) Henceforth the adversaries lose all power over him, since they no longer have access to his Christ-permeated ego.

The Foundation Stone of the Good

If we take the impending incarnation of Ahriman into consideration, together with all the trials associated with it which mankind will have to experience, the social relationships between people—in particular the need to cultivate on Earth human communities of an altogether new kind, whose foundation will be a purely spiritual impulse—acquire a special significance. Only such communities will be able effectively to withstand Ahriman when he appears on the Earth. Everything else in the social life of mankind will inevitably succumb to his magical power. For in the incarnation of Ahriman all the evil tendencies associated with the occult significance of 1998 are concentrated as though in a single earthly focus, with the result that it will be extremely difficult to withstand his alluring power.

This power of Satan-Ahriman, which tempts whole communities, great and small, is referred to in the Book of Revelation in the image of Gog and Magog (chapter 20, verses 7–8). Rudolf Steiner has this in mind when he speaks of 'the great act of seduction that Satan is planning in connection with Gog and Magog' (GA 346, 22 September 1924). He explains the significance of these apocalyptic images thus: 'A time will come when the

Satanic power will have made great efforts to win over humanity's powers of intelligence and when this Satanic power will have grown so great that it will approach all the groups that have formed; so the situation will really arise in which Satan's power will work into all the four corners of the world. These groups—smaller ones: Gog, and larger ones: Magog—will be exposed to temptation and seduction by the Satanic power'.

The only thing which will from the outset lie outside Ahriman's control is that spiritual and social sphere which will gradually be formed amongst mankind out of spiritual science: 'In spiritual science another sphere is created in which there is no Ahrimanic element. It is precisely by receiving in knowledge this spirituality to which the Ahrimanic powers have no access that man is strengthened to confront Ahriman *in the world*'.[55]

In this connection, the fact of Rudolf Steiner's founding the 'General Anthroposophical Society' at Christmas 1923 acquires a special significance; for this was a completely new social initiative springing wholly from the impulses of spiritual science. This true society of the Christmas Conference has the task in our time to make manifest to humanity an archetypal picture of a community of human beings which is not only capable of withstanding Ahriman as he comes in the flesh but also of bringing a completely new community-building principle to realisation in the world, one to which Ahriman will have no access. What is the nature of this principle?

When he appears in the West at the very beginning of

the next millennium, Ahriman, the unlawful 'prince of this world', will make his presence felt amongst mankind invested with immense power, authority and strength which he will rapidly extend to virtually all areas of modern civilisation. What Vladimir Solovyov described in general terms in his *A Short Story of Antichrist* will come about, namely, that everything that is subject to the powers of the world will inevitably come under his sway. The only things that will be able to escape his influence will be those that do not originate from this world and, hence, by their nature are inaccessible to the 'prince of this world'. In other words, only that which originates from Christ's kingdom and not from the realm of Ahriman will be capable of withstanding the latter's power.

Christ Himself pointed to this when He said: 'My Kingdom is not of this world.' (John 18:36) In one of his lectures Rudolf Steiner referred to those words as being 'significant and decisive' for our time, reckoning them as being among the 'fundamental words of Christianity, which shall pass through the whole world like holy impulses'.[56] However, Christ did indeed come to *this* world where 'the prince of this world' reigns, in order to strengthen within it His kingdom, which is 'not of this world' and to which for this reason Ahriman does not have access. Hence in another lecture from the same cycle Rudolf Steiner continues this thought as follows: 'Christ's kingdom is not of this world but it must work in this world, and human souls must make themselves the instruments of this kingdom which is not of this world.'[57] This means that, bearing in mind that the 'prince of this world', Ahriman, is shortly to incarnate, the most important task is to establish on Earth human communities into which he cannot enter, for at their foundation will be something which, in its origin, belongs to Christ's kingdom.

With this we have an entirely new community-forming principle which, from our time onwards, will gradually become the main and the only Christian social principle in earthly evolution as a whole. This is a principle of a human community which belongs entirely within *this* world amidst modern civilisation—inasmuch as its principal task (the overcoming of the 'prince of this world') lies within it—and which at the same time has as its inner foundation something that does not originate from this civilisation, in so far as the latter belongs to 'this world'.

This Foundation Stone of the Christmas Conference, which Rudolf Steiner also calls the 'dodecahedral imagination which has received its form through love',[58] originates from that etheric-imaginative realm in which Christ is now revealing Himself to mankind in a new, etheric form. Rudolf Steiner brought this Foundation Stone from the celestial land of Shambala which Christ has wholly renewed, a land whence all the true initiates of humanity have derived their forces for millennia,[59] and gave it to the Anthroposophical Society in order that this stone might become the spiritual foundation of its entire subsequent earthly activity, a foundation which the 'gates of hell' cannot overwhelm. (Matthew 16:18)

In giving this Foundation Stone to the Anthroposophical Society, Rudolf Steiner was opening up a new unique possibility for it in the future—which will come very soon indeed—of not succumbing to the Ahrimanic forces of the 'prince of this world' and thus of fulfilling its Michaelic task. However, the realisation of this possibility is associated with a serious trial that has stood before all anthroposophists since the Christmas Conference. This trial can be formulated as follows: whether their relationship to the Spirit has, through spiritual science, become sufficiently concrete that they are able to experience the purely supersensible Foundation Stone as something so real that they can stand both individually and as a community within the earthly world as on an unshakeable foundation. Only if the Anthroposophical Society endures this trial by basing its inner life upon this Foundation Stone can it gradually become an archetypal picture for mankind of a truly Christian community in the epoch of the consciousness soul, a community which is open to all the problems and vital questions of modern civilisation and which nevertheless has as its focus and firm foundation something coming directly from the spiritual world and, therefore, of a profoundly esoteric nature. Then the words with which the founder of the Anthroposophical Society formulated its principal task—for the sake of which it was brought into being at the Christmas Conference—will be able to come to fulfilment within it: 'We must be absolutely clear about the fact that our Society, before all others, will be given the task of combining the greatest conceivable openness with true and genuine esotericism'.[60] And Rudolf Steiner added that 'we must solve this fundamental problem ... in our hearts',[61] that is, where we have laid the Foundation Stone.

★

If we now turn our attention to the essential nature of this Foundation Stone, a remarkable perspective of altogether new possibilities of withstanding evil in the modern world opens up before our eyes.[62] At the Christmas Conference, Rudolf Steiner characterised the three main elements of the Foundation Stone in the following way: its substance consists of universal and human love, its form of universal and human imagination, and the spiritual light shining around it of universal and human thoughts. All three of its fundamental elements—light, imaginative form and substance of love—are present within it in two aspects: the macrocosmic and the microcosmic; and the essential nature of its activity within the human soul consists in the union of these two aspects.[63]

If one looks more attentively at the essential nature of these three elements of the Foundation Stone, one may discern in them the source of those spiritual forces with whose help it is possible today to withstand most effectively the assault upon humanity of all three kinds of opposing powers described at the beginning of this essay.

Turning again, therefore, to the activity of the Luciferic forces in our world, we must say: they always try to tempt man with the illusory world of fantasies, vague dreams and groundless visions, thus preventing him from finding that real ground under his feet which he needs in order to fulfil his mission on the Earth. This temptation may best be resisted through a clear and conscious human thinking which is imbued with the impulse of spiritual science rather than being materialistic and dead, that is, a thinking which, through spiritual science, can find the path to a universal thinking and, as a result of this, become a spiritual light in the supersensible world nearest to the Earth. Then the *light* of such a universal and human thinking, in which both human and angelic forces are working, will be able to overcome the power of Lucifer in the human soul. Similarly, Ahriman most of all fears true imaginations, in his efforts to allure man with the cold wisdom of the bare intellect. But when, with the help of spiritual science, man finds the path from human to cosmic imaginations, such universal and human *imaginations*—in which both human and archangelic forces are working—are capable of overcoming the power of Ahriman in his soul. Finally, by consciously developing within himself forces of love which, through spiritual science, are able gradually to gain access to the forces of cosmic love which have, as a result of the Mystery of Golgotha, entered fully into earthly evolution,[64] man will—as he experiences within his soul the working together of human forces and the forces of the Time-

Spirits (the Archai)—be in a position to overcome in his soul the power of the Asuric adversaries by means of this universal and human *love*.

All this can also be formulated as follows. Through inner work with the Foundation Stone such as has been described, human thoughts gradually find the path to the universal thoughts of the Angels, which can then help man to overcome the forces of Lucifer within him; similarly, human imaginations, through work with the Foundation Stone, find the path to the universal thoughts of the Archangels, which are able to overcome the forces of Ahriman; and finally, a purified and spiritualised love, when united with the forces of the Stone of Love, finds the path to the universal love of the Archai, which is capable of overcoming the power of Asur.

But this is still not all. The culmination of the Christmas Conference was not only the forming of the Foundation Stone out of the three elements that have been characterised but also the appearance in the 'light of thinking' surrounding it of the Spirit who is capable of leading those human beings who have laid this Foundation Stone in their hearts and souls into that kingdom of Christ, into that Shambala which He has renewed and where His etheric advent is now taking place. It follows from this that just as the three main elements of the Foundation Stone are able to protect the human soul from the three kinds of opposing spirits associated with our evolution—Lucifer, Ahriman and Asur—so the Spirit who enters our world directly from the Sun kingdom of Christ is similarly capable of overcoming the forces of the Sun demon in man's soul. For in the Spirit who is revealed in the radiant aura of the Foundation Stone we have the Helper ('Comforter') who has been sent down to us in our efforts to oppose the forces of Sorat. This is that Helper of whom we have a particular need at the time of the third appearance in the spiritual history of humanity of the number of the Beast. And so we must today oppose the shadowy influence of this number through the threefold being of the Foundation Stone and the Spirit who surrounds it, that Spirit who is capable of endowing us with the forces from the kingdom of the etheric Christ over which even the Sun demon himself is powerless.

All those elements of the Foundation Stone are also contained in the Foundation Stone Meditation, which is why it is a very powerful instrument in the battle with the opposing forces. If we bear in mind that within the hierarchy that is closest to man, the Third Hierarchy of the Angels, Archangels and Archai, the Angels represent—with respect to earthly humanity—also the two other categories of spirits belonging to this hierarchy, the Archangels and Archai, that is, the Third Hierarchy as a whole; that the Archangels represent the Second Hierarchy, the Exusiai (Powers), Dynamis (Principalities) and Kyriotetes (Dominions); and the Archai the First Hierarchy, the Thrones, Cherubim and Seraphim—this meditation will become for us an expression of the deepest spiritual essence of the Foundation Stone.

For the First, and highest, Hierarchy is headed by the Seraphim or the Spirits of universal *Love*; the Second Hierarchy is led by the Dominions or Spirits of Wisdom, that is, by the Sophian spirits who have sent man those forces which he needs in order to enter the world of *imaginations*; while the Third Hierarchy is guided by the Spirits of Time (Archai), the most important of whom in our epoch is Michael, the great ruler of the cosmic intelligence—the spiritual *light* of the creative thoughts of all the divine-spiritual hierarchies.

Thus all the three hierarchies who are invoked one after the other in the first three parts of the Foundation Stone Meditation respectively represent in our cosmos the forces of love, the forces of imagination (imaginative wisdom) and the forces of the (spiritual) light of thinking, that is, those very elements out of which Rudolf Steiner formed the Foundation Stone of the General Anthroposophical Society at the Christmas Conference. Hence the first three parts of the meditation, in their twofold micro-macrocosmic structure,* can help us respectively as follows: the first part, invoking all the beings of the

* The twofold structure of the Foundation Stone has a macro-microcosmic character, whereas in the Foundation Stone Meditation we have the opposite succession from the microcosm to the macrocosm. This difference is connected with the fact that the Foundation Stone is an objective phenomenon within the spiritual world, whereas the meditation associated with it is given to the individual human soul for its inner work, as a result of which the full spiritual reality of the Foundation Stone can be discerned.

First, highest Hierarchy, in the battle with the forces of Asur and his hosts; the second part, invoking all the beings of the Second Hierarchy, in the battle with the forces of Ahriman and the spirits who serve him; and the third part, addressed to all the beings of the Third Hierarchy, in the battle with Lucifer and those under his sway. For only the beings of the First Hierarchy can block Asur's path to our physical body, while the beings who represent them in the Third Hierarchy, the Archai (also called the Spirits of Personality), can protect us from his penetrating the consciousness soul; similarly, the spirits of the Second Hierarchy can block Ahriman's path to our etheric body, while the Archangels, who are their representatives in the Third Hierarchy, can help us to overcome his power in our intellectual or mind soul; finally, the spirits of the Third Hierarchy can together help us to prevent Lucifer from gaining access to our astral body, while their representatives, the Angels, can overcome his influence in the sentient soul.*

Finally, in the concluding, fourth part of the medita-

---

* In the present context, of course, it is not a question of a *total* overcoming of the opposing beings in the threefold soul but only of a vanquishing of that influence of theirs which is *destructive* for man's rightful evolution. This is even more the case with man's three 'bodily' sheaths (physical, etheric and astral bodies), in which the influence of the opposing beings can only be limited in the present epoch, that is, overcome only to a certain degree. Their eventual overcoming will be possible only at the end of the whole of earthly evolution, when man will have attained, respectively, the stages of the Spirit-Self, Life-Spirit and Spirit-Man.

tion we have a direct reference to that Spirit who can be revealed to us in his reality out of the radiant aura surrounding the Foundation Stone in the spiritual world. This fourth part of the meditation begins with the words:

> At the Turning Point of Time
> The Light of the World-Spirit
> Entered the stream of earthly being . . . ,

words which speak to us of that world *Spirit* who streamed into the whole of 'earthly being' as a result of the coming of Christ to the Earth and His union with it in the Mystery of Golgotha. Since that time this Spirit has been constantly at work in the whole of earthly evolution, though only in the present epoch of the consciousness soul has it been able for the first time to enter man's fully developed waking consciousness, which is to say, to penetrate his ego. In this sense, the Spirit who is revealed in the light of thinking of the 'dodecahedral Stone of Love' is that primordial Spirit who awakens and strengthens within man the forces of his individual ego and who was revealed to the world at Pentecost. Only now, in the new Christian mysteries, has this Spirit been revealed in the form in which it becomes for the first time accessible to *every* human being of good will who wants to lay the Foundation Stone of the Christmas Conference in his heart. And as this Spirit of the renewed Pentecost is at the same time the Spirit of the new social community, through it there can arise between human beings that *spiritual brotherhood* to which Christ Himself was referring when He said: 'For where two or three are gathered in my name, there am I in the midst of them.' (Matthew 18:20)

Then the inner experience of the Foundation Stone—imbued with this ego-awakening, and at the same time socially active, Spirit—will lead man to a real meeting with the etheric Christ in the supersensible sphere nearest to the Earth (the new Shambala). This will be possible because the principal constituent parts of the Foundation Stone as described above correspond precisely to the main elements of the Second Coming, when Christ appears to man as the Bearer of universal love, with His Form woven out of universal imaginations and a radiant aura of universal thoughts surrounding Him.[65]

All this can be further deepened in the following way. As the World Ego, Christ is clothed in three macrocosmic sheaths. His soul sheath consists of universal love, His etheric sheath of universal, imaginative wisdom, and His physical sheath* of universal light. For according to Rudolf Steiner, the true nature of the soul—when freed from all spirits of hindrance—is love, and the true nature of matter—when purified from all opposing forces—consists of the substance of pure, supersensible light;[66] while between them, as a mediating element, there work

* By the word 'physical' here is meant not a material but a supersensibly physical sheath. In this connection, Rudolf Steiner pointed out on more than one occasion that the nature of light is supersensible.

the forces of imaginative wisdom, or the forces of the Sophia.

These three fundamental elements, which are present both in the etheric appearance of Christ and in the Foundation Stone, correspond precisely to the inner structure of that new Sun which shall at some future time arise out of the transformed Earth. Its living seeds were implanted into earthly evolution as a result of the Mystery of Golgotha. Rudolf Steiner describes this as follows: 'We must understand that as we behold Christ dying on the Cross we are standing in the presence of the genesis of the new Sun.' For 'the death on the Cross becomes the seed whence a new Sun will be engendered'.[67] This new Sun, which has since then been in a constant process of becoming, consists of a spiritual focus—namely, the World Ego of Christ—and three sheaths which have been gradually forming themselves: universal love, in which the creative activity of Christ within Earth-existence is expressed; universal imagination, which gives the new Sun its wisdom-filled inner form; and the light of universal thoughts, which fashion its radiant body. Hence by implanting the Foundation Stone in the soil of his etheric heart and then continually working with it, every human being can become a conscious participant and helper in this as yet supersensible process of forming a new Sun, the foundation of the future cosmos of love.[68]

If this happens, the forces of the 'Sun of Christ' in Earth existence will be in a position both to defend and help us in the battle with the three aspects of evil and their cosmic source—the Sun demon. For this chief adversary of the human ego and all the Sun forces in our cosmos can be conquered, and eventually will be conquered, by the new moral Sun of the world which has attained its full spiritual strength, that Sun which is spoken of in the fourth part of the Foundation Stone Meditation:

> Light divine,
> Christ Sun ....

This can also be expressed as follows. In our time the etheric Christ appears to mankind enrobed in the supersensible sheaths of the new moral Sun of the world. Conscious work upon them with the help of the Foundation Stone therefore leads directly to an experience of the etheric Christ. This work consists of the following.

If a person today begins actively—with the help of spiritual science—to develop a capacity for a purely spiritual thinking, that is, if he truly endeavours to grasp the spiritual element in the world with his thoughts, these spiritualised thoughts—the spiritual light engendered by his thinking—will be able to ray forth into the spiritual world and lead him to their archetype, to those universal thoughts which now constitute the light-filled aura of the etheric Christ. And if, with the help of spiritual science, such a person gradually masters the capacity of transforming his thoughts into imaginations, that is, becomes inwardly creative, these human imaginations will also lead him to their archetype—to those universal imaginations out of which the spiritual form of the etheric Christ is woven. Then if, through spiritual science, he learns to perceive the whole world as being filled throughout with spirituality and at the same time experiences himself in his ego as a purely spiritual being, he will—by thus understanding his kinship with everything spiritual in the world—be able truly to love this world and all the beings who dwell in it. This pure, selfless human love will, moreover, eventually reveal to him its higher archetype in the spiritual world: the divine Bearer of the universal love, the Christ Himself, will appear before him.

The foundation of this inner path, leading from human thoughts, human imaginations and human love which form the three supersensible sheaths of the new moral Sun of the world, is contained in the twofold macro-microcosmic being of the Foundation Stone, which for this reason can also serve us as a gateway to experiencing the etheric Christ in our time.

It is possible to summarise the whole of the path which has been described as follows:

Foundation Stone	*Etheric Christ*
The Spirit, awakening the forces of the individual ego	The World Ego
Human love	Universal love
Human imagination	Universal imagination
The light of human thinking	Universal light

As a result, the human knowledge, human imagination and human love springing from Anthroposophy—qualities which form the inner essence of spiritualised science, art* and religion—will, for someone who has implanted the Foundation Stone into his soul, be able to become the guides to the etheric Christ, to His universal love, universal imagination and universal thoughts. Then the Christ Himself will send down to such an individual that 'universal Spirit' with whose help he will be in a position to withstand Sorat in the period of the third appearance of his number in earthly history.

This is the deeper significance of mankind's encounter with evil in the epoch of the consciousness soul. For 'if man did not open himself to these tendencies to evil, he would not succeed in acquiring the impulse in his consciousness soul [ie. in his individual ego] to receive into himself the Spirit of the universe, that Spirit which must henceforth fructify the whole sphere of cultural life if it is not to perish',[69] that is, fructify all three of its principal realms of science, art and religion.

★

Drawing the threads together, we can say: the foundation of the modern path to the etheric Christ is the *Foundation Stone of the Good*—given by Rudolf Steiner at the Christmas Conference—in its twofold nature, uniting

* The basis of any true art is man's capacity to live consciously or unconsciously in the world of imaginations.

man and the world, and also the meditation which relates to it. Because of their direct connection with the etheric Christ, they are each of the greatest importance today in the battle against *all* adversaries, both for the individual human being who has laid the Foundation Stone into his heart and is working intensively with the meditation and for a human community which is endeavouring to build its social life upon this foundation. For only by building upon it will we be able in future truly to withstand the ever strengthening forces of evil, to withstand them both as separate individualities and as a human community. If this happens, the General—that is, the universally human—Anthroposophical Society will be able to fulfil its principal task. It will manifest to the world a human community of an altogether new kind, in which humanity will gradually be able to behold a social archetype of what in a spiritual sense can alone protect it from a complete social catastrophe in the future, brought about by the subsequent growth of evil in earthly evolution.

A very powerful counterforce to evil in the social realm is contained in the Foundation Stone. However, it can be implanted in the soul only as a result of a free inner act, springing from man's ego and from the knowledge which he has won. Thus in the mystery of the Foundation Stone the individual and the universal are interconnected. For although the laying of the Stone is a purely individual deed, nevertheless in the human soul it is not only the means for personal development but above all—as Rudolf Steiner has particularly emphasised*—becomes *the Foundation Stone of a new human community*, where the principle of *spiritual brotherhood* can be fully realised for the first time.

The same principle also pervades the Foundation Stone Meditation. It begins with a threefold call to the individual soul ('soul of man') which has laid the Foundation Stone of the Christmas Conference into its soil, and concludes in the fourth part with a reference to that *common* deed which must follow from our union with the Spirit who is revealed in the light-filled aura of this 'dodecahedral Stone of Love':

That good may become
What we from our hearts would found
What we from our heads would direct
In conscious
Willing.

★

In setting the Foundation Stone of the Good over and against world evil, Rudolf Steiner was manifesting to humanity an archetypal picture of the overcoming of evil

* 'Let us ever remain aware of this Foundation Stone of the Anthroposophical Society which we have formed today', said Rudolf Steiner at the Christmas Conference (GA 260, 25 December 1923).

by good in the consciousness soul epoch in a purely Manichean spirit.* In this way he not only renewed the Manichean impulse but also united it with the Rosicrucian stream.

As a result we have in the New Mysteries a synthesis and further metamorphosis of the four streams of goodness: the Rosicrucian, the Manichean, the Grail stream and the stream of the Templars. However, they are all present in the New Mysteries not in an old but in a new form, renewed out of the modern Michaelic Spirit of the Age.

Thus the Rosicrucian stream has the aim of opening up to modern man the path of Christian initiation appropriate for the present consciousness soul epoch. Its focus and culmination is the encounter in the sphere of Intuition with the Christ, as the highest Representative of the divine 'I am'. In a spiritual sense true Rosicrucians are the successors of the mysteries of the Holy Grail.[70] At the threshold of the modern age these mysteries were preserved in the inner schools of the Rosicrucians. From

---

* The Manichean character of this deed of Rudolf Steiner's follows above all from the fact that the Foundation Stone and the meditation associated with it are a spiritual metamorphosis of the first Goetheanum, destroyed a year earlier by implacable enemies of the Spirit. This deed of the most radical forces of evil was transformed by Rudolf Steiner into a still greater good at the Christmas Conference. See further about the nature of the Manichean impulse in the life of Rudolf Steiner in the book by S.O. Prokofieff, *The Occult Significance of Forgiveness*, Temple Lodge Publishing 1995.

the Grail mysteries they derived their profound knowledge of the Christ Being and the universal significance of the Mystery of Golgotha. In a form renewed out of the Spirit of the Age, these Grail mysteries are present again in Anthroposophy. Hence Rudolf Steiner called the spiritual science which he founded a 'science of the Grail', and new initiates the 'initiates of the Grail'.[71]

The Manichean stream is also connected with the mysteries of the Holy Chalice. This relationship arises in particular from the fact that, according to Rudolf Steiner's spiritual-scientific research, the great founder of Manicheanism, Manes or Manu, became in one of his subsequent incarnations—under the name of Parsifal—the leading initiate of the Grail mysteries.[72] In Anthroposophy the Manichean stream was taken further in its development not only as a result of the deep penetration which Anthroposophy has made into the mystery of evil but above all through the new path of overcoming it opened up by spiritual science out of the forces of the etheric Christ.

Finally, a further stream to have flowed into the New Mysteries is that of the Templars, those medieval 'messengers' of the Holy Grail. In the idea of the threefolding of the social organism originating out of Anthroposophy, we have—in a form appropriate to the consciousness soul epoch—the rebirth of the innermost essence of the Templar stream: their endeavour to establish amongst mankind a new social structure in accordance with the modern thrust of the Christ impulse.

Thus in the New Mysteries we have:

The modern path of Christian initiation	—	the renewal of the Rosicrucian stream
Knowledge of the Christ and the Mystery of Golgotha	—	the renewal of the Grail mysteries
The understanding—and overcoming—of evil	—	the renewal of Manicheism
The threefolding of the social organism	—	the renewal of the Templar impulse

One can also trace the relationship of these four streams with the spiritual essence of the Foundation Stone. For this it is necessary to recall that the esoteric focus of the Grail mysteries is the appearance of the *Spirit* above the Holy Chalice. In order that evil may be transformed into good in the Manichean sense, a particularly strong power of *love* is needed ('love evil well', as the ancient Manichean principle says). A true resolution of humanity's social problems—as Rudolf Steiner has frequently indicated—can be arrived at only with the help of consciously unfolding *imaginations*. Finally, the Rosicrucian path of initiation—as the only one that is appropriate for the consciousness soul epoch—has as its foundation a complete spiritualisation of human thinking, which then becomes *light* in the spiritual world, thus enabling man to preserve his individual ego-consciousness as he enters the higher worlds. Hence the first stage of modern initiation is the 'study of spiritual science'.[73]

This can be summarised in the following way:

Foundation Stone		*New Mysteries*
Spirit	—	the renewed Grail stream
Love	—	the renewed Manichean stream
Imagination	—	the renewed Templar stream
Light of thinking	—	the renewed Rosicrucian stream

Henceforth these four streams of goodness work together, for they have a single source out of which they have been renewed—the New Mysteries of Anthroposophy. Their common foundation is the modern revelation of the etheric Christ, and the archetypal picture of their battle with evil is Michael's heavenly battle with the dragon.

With this we have indicated the main reason why the heavenly mysteries of Michael have been fully revealed for the first time through Anthroposophy precisely in our modern age. For it would be impossible rightly to encounter the forces of evil in the fifth post-Atlantean epoch and actively to withstand them without a spiritual relationship with Michael, which can be attained only as a result of a knowledge of his mission amongst mankind. In the spiritual worlds Michael is the highest guarantor of human freedom, and therefore a relationship with him can only be fully conscious, that is, founded upon a free knowledge of the Spirit through the individual ego.

Let us now turn to the imagination of Michael fighting the dragon, the central imagination of our time. In it, Michael, as the arch-deployer of all the heavenly forces and the Sun-countenance of Christ, opposes the dragon who represents the totality of all the evil spirits battling against the rightful course of evolution. John, the beloved disciple of Christ and the first Christian initiate, describes this battle in his prophetic book as follows: 'And war arose in heaven, Michael and his angels fighting against the dragon; and the dragon and his angels fought, but they did not prevail and there was no longer any place for them in heaven. And the great dragon was cast down, that ancient serpent, who is called the Devil and Satan, the deceiver of the whole world—he was cast down to the Earth, and his angels were cast down with him.' (Rev. 12: 7–9) In these words we have a reference to all three kinds of opposing forces through which the Sorat-dragon works in earthly evolution: the ancient serpent is Lucifer, who tempted mankind while still in Paradise, the Devil in this context is Ahriman and Satan is Asur.*

---

*See also Revelation 20:2. What has been said here is not at variance with the fact that, before Asur and his hosts entered into earthly evolution, Lucifer was in Christian tradition generally called the Devil and Ahriman Satan. Elsewhere in the Book of Revelation (ch.16: 13–14) we read: 'And I saw issuing from the mouth of the dragon and from the mouth of the beast and from the mouth of the false prophet three foul spirits like frogs. They are demonic spirits, performing signs, who go forth to the kings of the whole world to

In our time this heavenly battle of Michael with the dragon is being continued on Earth, among human beings; and in order that he may wage this battle in the consciousness soul epoch, man needs a real *knowledge* both of the forces of evil and of the Michaelic forces which oppose them, a knowledge which is now given to him in Anthroposophy. For only on the basis of such knowledge can he become a *conscious* collaborator and helper of Michael in this battle, upon whose outcome the entire future of earthly evolution depends. It is said of the victors in this battle: 'They have conquered him by the blood of the Lamb and by the word of their testimony, for they loved not their lives even unto death'. (v.11) The blood is the physical bearer of man's ego. The 'blood of the Lamb' is a picture of the universal 'I am' of Christ, of that higher cosmic power which, in union with the individual human ego, is capable of overcoming the might of all adversaries. The 'word of their testimony' is in our time the etheric advent of Christ proclaimed by

---

assemble them for battle...' This has to do with the last, decisive battle which all the demonic beings, together with those human beings who have succumbed to their influence, will wage against the true spirit. The three 'foul spirits' issuing from the mouth of the dragon or Sun demon are, respectively, Luciferic, Ahrimanic and Asuric beings. Furthermore, the 'dragon', 'beast' and 'false prophet' mentioned here refer—albeit from a somewhat different point of view—to the threefold countenance of the forces of evil: the 'dragon' works out of forces whose source lies beyond the bounds of earthly evolution, the 'beast' is already entering into it and the 'false prophet' appears directly amongst human beings.

spiritual science, the central spiritual event of the present epoch. While the voluntary repudiation of one's life, or soul, is, in the sense of the Christian mysteries, nothing other than the fulfilment of the words of the Apostle Paul: 'Not I, but Christ in me', (Galatians 2:20) that is, a person's conscious embarking upon the path of spiritual development which has become accessible to his consciousness soul through Anthroposophy, through its revelation of the divine Mysteries of the 'I am'.

As has already been shown, this path leads in our time to a direct experience of the etheric Christ; and the most important task of Anthroposophy is to proclaim Him to humanity. Rudolf Steiner spoke of this as follows: 'Here on Earth we must prepare for this event and create organs to perceive it. The new Christ event in the twentieth century—this is what we are now proclaiming ... Christ will be revealed to those people who with the help of spiritual science rise to an understanding, to a vision of the true Second Coming of Christ'.[74]

The whole of Michael's present activity in the supersensible world nearest to the Earth is directly connected with this etheric appearance of Christ. Rudolf Steiner indicates this in the following words:

> This appearance of [the etheric] Christ ... can take place only if Michael's rulership is extended ever more and more widely. This process is still going on in the spiritual world ... Michael is fighting on the plane which borders upon our world for the approach of [the etheric] Christ. He has need of his hosts, his champions.[75]

'This process is still going on in the spiritual world'—but from the end of the twentieth century it must also be continued by human beings on the Earth. For this purpose all true pupils of Michael must, at the threshold of the new millennium, be united around the spiritual Foundation Stone of the General Anthroposophical Society. For only by becoming unshakeably strengthened upon this foundation will they be able to extend Michael's rulership amongst mankind, that is to say, not only to withstand the power of evil in the modern world but also to begin truly to overcome it through the strength springing from their relationship with the etheric Christ.

'Michael needs a host of helpers who will bring the battle which he has already won on the astral plane to a conclusion on the physical plane. This is the great task which we must accomplish.'[76]

Appendix 1

The main elements of which the Foundation Stone consists are deeply connected with three tasks which modern man must accomplish on his path towards a personal encounter with the etheric Christ in the spiritual world. This is why the laying of the Foundation Stone in the human heart can lead one closer to the entire fullness of the supersensible reality of the Second Coming.

The first task consists of the spiritualisation of one's intellectuality, at whose foundation lies the Michaelic intelligence which has descended to the Earth. Its spiritualisation is necessary for a *conscious* beholding of Christ on the astral plane. Rudolf Steiner describes this process in the following words:

> Progress will only be made in this direction when a person develops this exalted intellectuality not merely for himself but also raises it up into the astral world. Through such an intellectual clairvoyance, the etherically visible Christ can and will approach those who are more developed in this sense more and more clearly over the course of the next three thousand years.[77] The whole path of anthroposophical knowledge, as described in *Knowledge of the Higher Worlds*,[78] has the aim of developing just such 'intellectual clairvoyance'.

In this respect, the pupil of spiritual science can be especially helped through inner work with the light of thinking of the Foundation Stone. This light can become for him a kind of beacon in the process of transforming his intellectuality, for it is capable of unfolding those qualities which his thinking needs to possess in order rightly to enter the spiritual (astral) world. Pre-eminent among those qualities is the *morality* of thinking, which he must not only cultivate within himself but also learn to perceive with his heart, as a new organ of knowledge. Rudolf Steiner describes this condition as follows: 'He thinks indeed with his head, but his heart feels the brightness of the thought or its shade'.[79]

Once he has imparted this inner moral strength to his thinking, he finds that the light inherent in his thinking is related in its nature to the radiant aura around the Foundation Stone. Then the—at once—universal and human thoughts living within it will indicate to him a further path through which he will be able to unite his earthly thoughts with the universal thoughts of the Angels and thus awaken in his soul the capacity to behold the *light* (the radiant aura) of the etheric Christ.

The second task consists in widening the inner space of his conscience to such an extent that it can in time take on an imaginative character in his soul. As a result an altogether new faculty will develop in his soul, which will consist in his being able to 'see in pictures [imaginations] the effects of his deeds for the future'.[80] Then he will be guided in his moral conduct no longer by an abstract voice of conscience but by a concrete vision of spiritual pictures of what he must accomplish in his life in order to rectify his past mistakes. And a conscience that has become imaginative will open the way for a right (moral) experience of an *imagination* of the etheric Christ, the Representative of the cosmic conscience and the source of all moral intuitions.

If the Foundation Stone—in which human and cosmic imaginations are united—is implanted in the soil of his etheric heart, this can represent a significant help towards such a transformation of conscience into a new imaginative faculty. Through it, the imaginative forces of the cosmos springing from the sphere of the Archangels will be able to permeate his entire soul-life, even to the extent of changing the inner character of his conscience.

As for the third task, it is most fully expounded by Rudolf Steiner in the lecture entitled 'How can I find the Christ?'[81] In this lecture Rudolf Steiner speaks of one very important condition of the experience of Christ in our time. This condition consists in every contemporary human being passing through a state of complete inner powerlessness with regard to his personal aspirations, and at the same time being able to live in this state without falling into despair or trying to defend himself from it by self-deception and illusions.

The only power in the human soul which is really capable of enduring this trial by powerlessness is the power inherent in the individual human ego, when it has been imbued with a pure and selfless love for the Spirit: a love which is still human but which has already been touched by a heavenly ray of divine (universal) love. Only if *such* a love—like a never-dying flame, warming the entire soul—is present in a human being even in the state of total powerlessness, the experience of this state will eventually be followed by the resurrection from it which is associated with the direct revelation of the Christ forces in the human soul. Thus in the lecture referred to, Rudolf Steiner particularly emphasises that in our time only an individual who out of his personal experience 'can speak of these two experiences, of powerlessness and of the resurrection from powerlessness, is speaking of a real experience of Christ'.

The 'imaginative Stone of Love', with its twofold macro-microcosmic nature, can be of immeasurable help also in this trial. For in its substance are united the forces of human and universal love streaming from the realm of the Archai or the Spirits of Personality. If, therefore, the Foundation Stone becomes the unshakeable foundation of a person's entire life of soul, he will be able to erect on this foundation a bridge between powerlessness and the resurrection from powerlessness, thereby embarking upon the path leading from human to the universal *love* in which the Christ is revealed.

To sum up what has been said:

Three fundamental experiences on the path towards perceiving the etheric Christ

1. Morality of knowledge	—	the light of thinking of the Foundation Stone
2. Visionary Conscience	—	the imaginative form of the Foundation Stone
3. Powerlessness and the resurrection from powerlessness	—	the substance of love of the Foundation Stone

Only by fulfilling the three tasks referred to can man develop within himself the inner forces capable of effectively withstanding the various categories of spirits of evil. Thus the Luciferic beings in our time try in every possible way to separate the sphere of knowledge from the sphere of human morality,* with the object of turning man into a moral automaton who is completely dependent in all moral and spiritual questions upon outward authority, and who in his knowledge is increasingly inclined either towards a nebulous religiosity or towards materialistic science and sometimes to both of these at once.

* Rudolf Steiner says that in 'Copernicanism is contained one of the last ... great attacks which Lucifer has launched against human evolution' (GA 130, 18 December 1930). For in the transition from the Middle Ages to modern times it has been the teachings of Copernicus which have given the main impulse towards separating human conceptions of the cosmos from the moral principle working within it.

As for the Ahrimanic forces, their dominant influence amongst mankind can be opposed particularly by the forces of the imaginative conscience stirring within man, a conscience which leads him to a more conscious experience and direct fulfilment of his individual karma. This is what Ahriman fears most of all, for he well knows that 'the good spirits have given [man] the possibility of karma in order to withstand the Ahrimanic powers'.[82]

Finally, the Asuric spirits will especially endeavour to invoke in man a feeling of total powerlessness before the outer and inner problems besetting him from all sides, problems which will increasingly appear to him to be insoluble. And at the same time these spirits will seek in every possible way to prevent man from escaping from this state of inner powerlessness, inasmuch as the resurrection from it is connected with the experience of the etheric Christ. In contrast, they will by all means available to them try to thrust man into an abyss of despair and a second moral death, the consequence of which will be the incurable sickness and, ultimately, the gradual extinction of all earthly culture. For 'the sickness of culture and the death of culture' is the terrible 'gift of the Asuras' to modern humanity,[83] if it is not directed before it is too late towards those impulses of human evolution which are capable not only of preventing earthly culture from wholly succumbing to the forces of death but also of leading it to a real resurrection from that state of powerlessness in which it now finds itself.

This feeling of general powerlessness will grow particularly from our time onwards. For Christ's appearance in an etheric form must necessarily be preceded by a general experience that the spiritual, social and cultural values inherited by humanity from the past are no longer able to sustain man, still less show him the path into the future. Rudolf Steiner speaks of this as follows:

> But before this happens [the etheric appearance of Christ], all the vestiges of the old must be turned into total nothingness ... But out of this nothingness man must find his true freedom. The new beholding [of Christ] must be born out of this nothingness. Man must discover in this nothingness a new strength. Spiritual science would seek to prepare him for this.'[84]

In this sense the *whole* of Anthroposophy is a contribution towards this preparation. For it represents a real power that is capable of overcoming this state of powerlessness and this ever greater plunge into nothingness and of leading humanity to rebirth in a new, free and conscious spiritual life. The actual paths leading to this goal have already been spoken of in the present essay. Of primal importance in this respect is inner work with the spiritual Foundation Stone, which was laid by Rudolf Steiner at the founding of the General Anthroposophical Society at the Christmas Conference in 1923/1924.

Appendix 2

After the lectures whose content forms the basis of the present essay, the author was asked a question as to how it is possible to reconcile Rudolf Steiner's indication that the three spirits of evil referred to—Lucifer, Ahriman and Asur with their hosts—belong to the beings of the Third Hierarchy and are, respectively, retarded Angels, Archangels and Archai[85] with the fact that Rudolf Steiner spoke on more than one occasion about the existence of retarded spirits (Luciferic and Ahrimanic) also among the beings of the Second and even the First Hierarchy.[86]

In order to answer this question, it is necessary to recall once more that the three kinds of beings forming the Third Hierarchy which is closest to man—the Angels, Archangels and Archai—are at the same time the representatives within this Third Hierarchy of all three hierarchies. This can be explained in the following way:

Third Hierarchy

Angels (Guardian Angels)	representatives of the Third Hierarchy	{ Angels Archangels Archai

Archangels (Folk Spirits)	representatives of the Second Hierarchy	Spirits of Form Spirits of Movement Spirits of Wisdom
Archai (Time Spirits)	representatives of the First Hierarchy	Spirits of Will Cherubim Seraphim

It follows from this that the higher members of the Third Hierarchy, the Archangels and Archai, are connected with man by and large through the mediation of the Angels who serve them and who have the task of guiding the individual karma of a human being in accordance with the karma of his people and his time. However, in addition to working through angelic beings, the Archangels and Archai can under certain circumstances exert an influence upon man's inner life also directly by entering right into his soul. Hence in the published version of the Foundation Stone Meditation Rudolf Steiner calls all three categories of spirits of the Third Hierarchy the 'Spirits of Soul', that is, hierarchic beings who work within the human soul and guide it.

In contrast, the beings belonging to the Second Hierarchy—the Spirits of Form, the Spirits of Movement and the Spirits of Wisdom—do not enter directly into the human soul. Their spiritual forces are too great for the human soul to be able to endure their presence and avoid becoming disorientated. They therefore work directly only in man's *bodily* sheaths, where he is completely unconscious of their activity. This is even more the case with the beings of the First Hierarchy—the Spirits of Will, the Spirits of Harmony (Cherubim) and the Spirits of Love (Seraphim). In order to exert an influence upon the human soul they make use of their representatives in the Third Hierarchy—the spirits of the Second Hierarchy utilising the Archangels and the spirits of the First Hierarchy the Archai.

If we compare the nature of all three hierarchies we can say: the Third Hierarchy enters directly into man's soul life, inasmuch as without this the individual guidance of human beings (Angels), the guidance of peoples (Archangels) and the guidance of successive historical epochs (Archai) would all be impossible. The Second Hierarchy does not enter into the human soul; it only works in the objective natural world (and also in the human body, inasmuch as it is a part of the latter). In all the phenomena of nature around us, and also in the planets of our solar system and the Sun itself, the creative activity of the Second Hierarchy is manifested. The beings of the First Hierarchy are still higher. Their all-encompassing activity is not merely confined to the solar system. They work within the entire cosmos, creating and ruling over countless worlds within it.

With all that has been said we have the necessary preparation to answer the question that was raised. Rudolf Steiner actually speaks of the presence of retarded beings amongst all the hierarchies. However, only retarded beings of the *Third* Hierarchy can enter directly into man's inner being—that is, only Luciferic,

Ahrimanic and Asuric spirits. By penetrating his soul they become very powerful moral tempters, inclining him—in the case of Lucifer—to pride and arrogance, to falsehood and fear (Ahriman) and to misanthropy and senseless cruelty (Asur).

The spirits of the Second Hierarchy—despite their being higher than the Third Hierarchy—cannot approach man from within as moral tempters in the present period of world evolution, inasmuch as the main field of their activity is outer nature: they do not enter the human soul. How, then, are the negative influences of retarded spirits of this Second Hierarchy manifested? We find them in phenomena such as earthquakes, volcanic eruptions, floods, fires and other natural catastrophes. They all bring to man immense suffering, misfortunes and at times even physical death and annihilation. However, it is completely apparent that, despite all the negative consequences of the natural catastrophes which they bring about, their activity cannot be compared with those *moral* temptations which derive from the retarded beings of the Third Hierarchy. With respect to man the activity of beings of the Second Hierarchy (and even more so of the First) is natural as opposed to moral. (It can become moral—that is, conscious—only through initiation.)

In this sense, the battle against evil in the earthly aeon has only to do with retarded beings of the Third Hierarchy. Only in the future incarnations of our cosmos—on Jupiter, Venus and Vulcan and so forth—will man have to take a conscious part in opposing the evil forces deriving from the spheres of higher hierarchies. The only being belonging to a higher hierarchy than the Third who is nevertheless capable of having a destructive influence upon man's whole inner (moral) world is Sorat, the Sun demon. However, his essential nature and cosmic origin remain a mystery which neither the Book of Revelation nor the spiritual-scientific research of Rudolf Steiner reveal. In his lectures on the Apocalypse there is merely an indication that 'Sorat is the name of the Sun demon and the antagonist of the Lamb'.[87] From this it is possible to draw the conclusion that in the spiritual world he opposes mainly the Second or *Sun* Hierarchy, the beings of which hierarchy are called the 'Spirits of Light' in the Foundation Stone Meditation. Furthermore, as the chief opponent of the 'ego-principle' in our cosmos, Sorat especially acts counter to the Sun Elohim or Spirits of Form, who endowed man with his individual ego at the beginning of earthly evolution. Having said this, neither the question of Sorat's origin nor that of the nature of his being have been in any sense resolved.

The reason why Rudolf Steiner did not reveal this mystery can be discerned in that, for as long as Sorat works within earthly evolution only through the three categories of the spirits of opposition who serve him, he does not enter into it himself. His first direct penetration into it—an event of which the Book of Revelation speaks so clearly—will most likely take place around

AD 2664, when the number of the Beast will appear for the *fourth* time in human historical development.

For on the first occasion that this happened, the activity of Sorat was fully directed towards the physical plane and came to expression in the use which he made of the Academy of Gondhishapur, which actually existed on Earth in the seventh century. On the second occasion, when the Order of Templars was destroyed, his activity bore a more etheric character. At that time Sorat's Ahrimanic demons—speaking through the tortured knights—were making use of their etheric bodies, which were temporarily deprived of their connection with their egos. In the twentieth century, however, in connection with the third appearance of the apocalyptic number, the Beast from the abyss is mainly working on the astral plane, though now he is for the first time not only using Luciferic and Ahrimanic spirits for his invasion of humanity—as formerly—but also Asuric spirits.

Finally, in the period of the fourth appearance of the apocalyptic number in earthly evolution, the Sun demon will try to attack the human ego, not only through the mediation of Asuric beings but also through his own power. In order that this future trial may be endured, there will by that time have to be a sufficient number of people who have consciously experienced a meeting with the etheric Christ and have as a result so strengthened their individual egos through the forces of the World Ego of Christ that all Sorat's temptations will have no power over them. By then the mystery of his cosmic origin will also have been revealed to humanity.

However, the encounter with Sorat in the second half of the third millennium will not be the final battle with him. This will take place in a far more distant future, when mankind will possess *spiritual powers* in full measure and will therefore have the possibility of using them in the sense of Christ or misusing them in the sense of the Sun demon who opposes Him. At that time the opposition in earthly evolution between the human beings engaging in white and black magic will lead to the eventual division of humanity into good and evil. Then the human beings who have consciously chosen the 'black path' will wholly give themselves up to Sorat and his demons and will therefore form the 'retarded' humanity of the earthly aeon, bearing upon themselves the imprint of the number of the Beast. For 'in the mystery of 666 or the mystery of Sorat is hidden the secret of black magic'.[88]

Thus it will be possible to withstand Sorat in this apocalyptic future only with the forces of true 'white magic', whose source will be the forces of the Sun logos, which entered into earthly evolution through the Mystery of Golgotha.

TWO

The Mysteries of the Shepherds and the Kings in the Light of Anthroposophy[1]

Rudolf Steiner spoke in the following words from one of his lectures about the direct participation of the Sophia in the events of the Turning Point of Time: 'Through the revelation to the poor shepherds in the field, through the revelation to the Magi from the East there worked the divine Sophia, the Heavenly Wisdom'. How are we to understand this statement by the spirit-researcher of modern times?

In order to answer this question we shall first turn to the spiritual history of mankind. As we know, Anthroposophy speaks about two great mystery-streams which in former times made their way to the East from the ancient continent of Atlantis. From a geographical point of view they can be characterised as a northern and a southern stream. In the northern stream the mysteries that were cultivated were mainly those where the endeavour was to penetrate into the spiritual world by breaking through the veil of outward sense-perceptions; while in the southern stream the pupils in the mysteries strove to enter the spiritual world by penetrating behind the veil of inner soul-experiences.

Rudolf Steiner characterised the main distinctive qualities of these two kinds of mysteries through the example of two great initiates of earthly evolution, who attained the highest stages of development in them. One of these initiates was Gautama-Buddha, who attained enlightenment on the path of the southern mysteries and rose from the stage of Bodhisattva to that of Buddha; while the other was the great Zarathustra, who attained the highest initiation on the path of the northern mysteries, as a result of which he became worthy of receiving the revelations of the Sun Spirit Himself, the divine Ahura-Mazdao, thus becoming the first in post-Atlantean times to experience the cosmic Christ before His coming to the Earth. In this way, both initiates—albeit on different paths—became the servants of the central spiritual Being of our cosmos, the Christ.

The need for *two* mystery-streams in earthly evolution has its origin in a definite cosmic law. According to this law, if a new impulse capable of raising evolution to the next, higher stage is to appear within it, a certain polarity—in the form of two polar streams—has first to manifest itself in the cosmos. Within such streams altogether different qualities and capacities can gradually be developed to the point where they can subsequently be united on a higher plane, which is necessary if a new, higher impulse is to be born within earthly evolution. Thus according to this law, in the evolution of the cosmos there first took place the separation of the Sun from the Earth, and then the separation between the Earth and the Moon. In subsequent times, however, they will be reunited, though at a more perfected level.

This law is also the reason for the arising of the two main streams—the northern and the southern—of the pre-Christian mysteries. For their independent development and subsequent union was necessary in order to prepare for the central event of earthly evolution, the incarnation on Earth of the divine Being of the Christ and His passing through the Mystery of Golgotha. 'For where two or three are gathered in my name, there am I in the midst of them' (Matthew 18:20)—these words of Christ Jesus are a direct reference to the aforesaid law of the spiritual world, which works on all levels of existence.

Thus it was the subsequent incarnation on Earth of the Christ Being which made it necessary that the two mystery-streams referred to came into being on ancient Atlantis, inasmuch as only through their interaction and higher synthesis could the conditions necessary for this event be created. And so if we turn to the events of the Turning Point of Time as described in the Gospels, we find that these two streams play a direct part in them. In the simple shepherds in the field who figure in the Gospel of St. Luke and the wise Magi of whom St. Matthew's Gospel relates, we have the chosen representatives at the Turning Point of Time of both the mystery-streams of antiquity.

The cosmic law referred to also has a further significance which is of importance for our theme. For wherever there is a union of opposites, where in place of opposition and rivalry there arises the harmony of oneness, this is a manifestation of the forces of that sublime spiritual being who in Christian esotericism is called the divine Wisdom or the Sophia. In Russian there is one word which refers to this particular quality of the Sophia, a word which is used for the human virtue most closely associated with her. This word is 'tselomudriye' [literally 'chastity'; however, the word is composed from 'tselo' = whole, intact and 'mudrost' = wisdom]. Wisdom as understood by the genius of the Russian language is always whole and indivisible. It unites everything and leads to a higher harmony.

In this we have the foundation for understanding Rudolf Steiner's words about the direct participation of the heavenly Sophia in the two streams of the shepherds and the kings. In so far as both these streams were to come together at the Turning Point of Time, the forces of the Sophia were working in them leading them to this union.

But how did this union come about? In order to arrive at an answer to this question, it is necessary to dwell at greater length on the character of the initiation received by the kings on the one hand and by the shepherds on the other.

★

According to Christian tradition, the Magi came to Palestine at the Turning Point of Time from Persia. For at that time, Persia with its mysteries, which had been founded by the great Zarathustra himself, was the cradle of all the magical knowledge of mankind. And when the Gospel tells us that the Wise Men from the East who came to worship the child born in Bethlehem were *Magi*, this is a direct reference to the source of their initiation as being in the mysteries of ancient Persia.

There is also no doubt that their journey of many months from Persia to Palestine was preceded by years of preparation in the mysteries, whence they derived their deep spiritual wisdom. This mystery-wisdom came to expression above all in their clairvoyant faculties of imaginative perception of the spiritual world, faculties which enabled them to behold the 'star of Bethlehem', their guide to the place of the new birth of their teacher, Zarathustra,* who incarnated in Palestine in order to prepare for the divine Christ Being's coming to the Earth.

Thus their path to the place of the central event of earthly evolution was a long one in both a spatial and a temporal sense. Moreover, they had to be prepared for their mission at the Turning Point of Time in their previous incarnations, of which modern spiritual science has the following to say. In the sixth pre-Christian century, approximately at the time when Gautama-Buddha was living and working in India, Zarathustra was also incarnated on Earth. He was living at that time in Babylon under the name of Zaratos or Nazaratos, and, as

* In Greek—Zoroaster, which when translated means 'shining' or 'golden star'.

an esoteric teacher, had many pupils. Three of the most advanced of these subsequently incarnated on Earth in ancient Persia as the three Magi from the East.

Rudolf Steiner tells us the name of only one of them in that time. This is the individuality of the Greek philosopher and initiate Pythagoras. His visit to Babylon and the initiation that he received there from the great Nazaratos is mentioned in virtually all the descriptions of his life that have come down to us. Rudolf Steiner does not tell us the names of the other two pupils of Zaratos. However, it is not difficult to find out who they were from historical sources. One of them was the Hebrew prophet Daniel who was living in Babylon, while the other was the Persian king Cyrus who—remarkably for those times—conquered Babylon without the shedding of blood.

If one compares these three pupils of Nazaratos, one discovers that each of them received from him a quite particular initiation. Pythagoras, as a philosopher, received an initiation into the mysteries of cosmic thinking; Daniel, as a prophet, into the mysteries of cosmic feeling; and the Persian King Cyrus into the mysteries of cosmic will. All three pupils then brought the fruits of these initiations into their next incarnation at the Turning Point of Time, when they appeared in Persia in order to pay homage to their reincarnated teacher and give a symbolically real indication of his new mission. This mission was to prepare the three earthly sheaths—the physical, etheric and astral bodies—for the descent into them of the Christ Being at the Baptism in the Jordan.

In this sense the gifts brought by the Magi are above all a symbolic indication of those higher qualities of thinking, feeling and will with whose help the ego of Zarathustra was to purify and spiritualise the three sheaths of Jesus for the receiving of the Christ Being. Thus gold was an indication of the forces of thinking, which purify the astral body; frankincense of the forces of feeling, which purify the etheric body; and myrrh of the will-forces, which purify the physical body. In other words, the gifts spoke of those three sheaths which Zarathustra was to sacrifice to the Christ as He descended from the spiritual worlds, sacrificially leaving them at the Baptism in the Jordan.

The path followed by the shepherds at the Turning Point of Time was completely different. It was neither of long duration nor over a wide area, for their pastures lay not far from Bethlehem, and in their simple and unsophisticated manner of life we do not at first find any hint of initiation. But what does Rudolf Steiner's spiritual research tell us about them? In the poor shepherds in the field, he says, the forces of the Hebrew prophets were reborn. This means that those spiritual qualities which the ancient Hebrew people was to develop over the centuries in order to fulfil its chief mission—the fashioning of the earthly sheaths for the coming of the divine Messiah—were manifested in them with a particular power. What were these qualities? Rudolf Steiner characterises them in terms of a quite special capacity to experience moral impulses in the realm of the will.

Whereas the heathen cultures—in so far as they had their sources in the ancient mysteries—were based on the element of *wisdom*, the ancient Hebrew culture, in contrast, from the very beginning of its existence had as its foundation the element of *will*, although this was at that time still guided from without with the help of commandments and other outer restrictions. This is the source of the deep antipathy running right through all the centuries of the Hebrew people's existence towards anything heathen or 'unclean', anything which in one way or another was connected with the polytheism of nature-wisdom.

Thus the emergence of the Hebrew people is associated with its forefather Abraham's leaving the town of Ur in Chaldea, where there was an ancient mystery-centre in which the cosmic (stellar) gods in particular were worshipped, and with his journey to Palestine in order to establish a new people there which, with the help of a very strict monotheism, was above all to develop moral will-forces capable without the slightest hesitation of following the higher voice of Jahveh, as was most strongly the case with the ancient Hebrew prophets.

But who were these mighty spiritual individualities? When speaking about the Old Testament prophets, Rudolf Steiner made it clear that, in them, individualities were incarnating amongst the ancient Hebrew people who in their past earthly lives had been initiates of different mysteries of wisdom of the heathen peoples. However, when they appeared amongst the people of Israel, they sacrificially renounced all the wisdom which they had gathered in their past incarnations as a result of their participation in the ancient mysteries, in order unconditionally to follow the inspirations of Jahveh alone.

The same can be said of the poor shepherds in the field near Bethlehem. They too, like the ancient Hebrew prophets, belonged in their past incarnations to various mysteries of the wisdom of humanity. However, for the fulfilment of their mission at the Turning Point of Time they sacrificially renounced this wisdom and incarnated on Earth as simple shepherds,* in order to receive the Christ impulse directly into their will-forces.

Thus in contrast to the Magi, who had to follow a long path of initiation into the wisdom of the Persian mysteries, the shepherds did not have any special wisdom in their day consciousness. But when the choir of angels appeared to them in revelation and the voice directly addressing the forces of their moral will sounded from the spiritual world, they obeyed it unquestioningly and without hesitation and immediately set off on their way. In other words, from the outset they perceived the divine

---

* Similarly, some of the Apostles were poor fishermen who had temporarily renounced the spiritual wisdom which they had gathered in previous incarnations.

revelation not in the form of wisdom but as a force which directly penetrated their will. And so, despite receiving their revelations only at the very last moment, by obeying them without hesitation they were nevertheless able to participate in the events of the Turning Point of Time in common with the Magi, who had known about them from mystery-wisdom long before their arrival in Palestine.

Thus the path of the shepherds was short both spatially (in that they were in a field not far from Bethlehem) and temporally, but it led no less directly to the goal than did the long path of the Magi.

★

The deep wisdom contained in the interaction of both paths, and in their eventual union in a single process of preparation for the appearance on Earth of the divine Christ Being, is a testimony to the direct participation in the events of Palestine of the heavenly Wisdom—the Sophia.

There is much evidence that knowledge of her always existed in ancient Hebrew esotericism and in the Babylonian mysteries in which Zarathustra had initiated the three Magi from the East in their previous incarnations. Thus in the Wisdom of Solomon one can find a whole series of references to her. She is also spoken of in Ecclesiasticus, the Book of Jesus, son of Sirach. And the Mystery-tradition of Chaldea and Babylon speaks of the mighty Archangel Marduk-Michael as being the son of a still higher cosmic being Ea or Ia, whose name, when joined to the predicate 'that which has being' or—in the mystery-language of those times—'soph', reveals to us the secret of this special being of the spiritual world, the divine Sophia. Thus the Sophia, the divine wisdom, worked in a heavenly, anticipatory way in the destinies of both the shepherds and the kings.

There is a reference to this mystery of the working of the Sophia at the Turning Point of Time in the fourth, concluding part of the Foundation Stone Meditation, given by Rudolf Steiner at the Christmas Conference of 1923. It begins as follows:

> At the Turning Point of Time
> The Light of the World-Spirit
> Entered the stream of earthly being.
> Darkness of night
> Had held its sway.
> Day-radiant Light
> Poured into the souls of men.
> Light
> That gives warmth
> To simple shepherds' hearts,
> Light
> That enlightens
> The wise heads of kings...

In these lines the word 'light' is mentioned four times. The first of these references, according to the Dutch anthroposophist Zeylmans van Emmichoven, relates to the being of the Sophia ('the Spirit-Light of the World'), the second to her 'son', the Archangel Michael, who overcame the darkness of unknowing and works as a mediator between the Sophia and mankind.*

This light originating from the Sophia and working through her 'son', Michael, spiritually guided the destinies of both the shepherds and the kings, and enabled them both to accomplish their mission in full measure at the Turning Point of Time—that of together preparing for the incarnation of the Christ on Earth.

*

When this sublime event takes place, the Christ Himself begins to shine in their souls, filling them with a new *light* of wisdom and an inner *warmth* of love which permeates their thoughts and transforms their wills. Henceforth the shepherds and the kings are together in a position to unite both qualities—the light of wisdom and the warmth of love—in full harmony in their being, that is, to bring the forces of the head and the forces of the heart into complete concord.

This cardinal change which has taken place in both mystery streams under the direct influence of the power of Christ is reflected in the following lines of the fourth part of the Foundation Stone Meditation:

---

* In the ancient Hebrew mysteries he was venerated as the guiding spirit of the people of Israel, while in Babylon the main temple where Nazaratos lived and taught in the sixth century was dedicated to him under the name of Marduk.

Light Divine
Sun of Christ!
Warm Thou
Our hearts,
Enlighten Thou
Our heads.

In these lines we have a reference to the harmonious union of both mystery streams as a result of the dawning of the Sun of Christ in earthly evolution. For henceforth the 'divine light' of Christ permeates both the hearts of the shepherds and the heads of the kings, uniting both kinds of mysteries in the new, united mysteries of esoteric Christianity. This is also a higher archetype of the entire subsequent mystery-evolution of humanity, an archetype which is to be brought to realisation by *every* human being in full freedom within his own soul.

In other words, since the Mystery of Golgotha every human individual has himself to unite in his soul the stream of the shepherds and the stream of the kings, by permeating both his heart and his head with the power of Christ. This means that all those who in the past belonged to the stream of the shepherds must in the Christian epoch develop within themselves the capacities of the kings, while those who in former times were connected more with the mysteries of the kings must now develop within themselves the qualities of the shepherds. The essence of this thought can be expressed in the following mystery-formula: henceforth the shepherds must become kings, and the kings shepherds.

In the Christmas lectures in 1920 which he gave in Dornach, Rudolf Steiner spoke at some length about this metamorphosis of the two spiritual paths under the direct influence of the Christ impulse. In these lectures he indicated that the endeavour to fulfil this new mystery-ideal is in an esoteric sense none other than a quest for the new Isis, the divine Sophia, who is alone capable of giving modern man a true *knowledge* of Christ. Rudolf Steiner spoke about this as follows: 'Then ... through this power of the divine Sophia ... will the Christ, who since the Mystery of Golgotha has been united with Earth-existence, be able rightly to work within man, for He will be truly recognised. It is not Christ that we lack; the knowledge of Christ, ... the Sophia of Christ is what we lack.'

Later in the same lecture, Rudolf Steiner spoke about this quest for the new Isis, the divine Sophia, as being the most urgent task of the anthroposophical movement, and he referred to the Anthroposophical Society as a community of modern seekers of the Sophia who are united by their common wish to serve this high spiritual being. This *collective quest* for higher spiritual wisdom must become the central, community-forming principle of the Anthroposophical Society, one that is able to unite all its members in a common love for the divine Wisdom, the Sophia. 'It could be', said Rudolf Steiner, 'that this Anthroposophical Society could become a community of human beings united in love, because of the quest which they feel themselves to have in common. Let us become conscious of this most intimate of inner tasks!'

How can this quest become a reality in the human soul, how can this union of the qualities of the shepherds and the kings come about, how can a complete harmony of the forces of head and heart be attained? Rudolf Steiner described this as follows.

The shepherds must now spread that warmth of heart which they once inwardly brought to meet the voice from the higher worlds—that voice which brought tidings to them in the field of the approach of the great event in Palestine—throughout outer nature, by experiencing the latter as the great revelation of the new Spirit of the Earth, that is, of the Christ Himself since His union with earthly evolution as a result of the Mystery of Golgotha. The modern shepherds must perceive the voice of Christ Himself in all the processes of nature.

On the other hand, the kings must bring those spiritual imaginations which they formerly beheld only outwardly, in the expanses of the cosmos—in whose heights the Christmas star appeared to them—into their own inner world, by developing within themselves new inner imaginations. Imagination of this latter kind can be found above all in the mighty pictures of world evolution contained in many lectures and in the fundamental books of Rudolf Steiner.

When an individual of modern times receives into his soul the spiritual-scientific imaginations of world evolution, describing as they do the cosmic conditions of Old

Saturn, Old Sun, Old Moon, the Earth and the future aeons of Jupiter, Venus and Vulcan, he is thereby entering upon the new path of the kings. And when anyone today immerses himself in a Goetheanistic knowledge and experience of the natural world around him, when, in Rudolf Steiner's words, the laboratory table becomes for him an altar, he is embarking upon the new path of the shepherds.

'Matter is built up in the way in which the Christ has gradually formed it [since the Mystery of Golgotha]':[2] in these words the highest ideal of the new knowledge of the shepherds will come to be enshrined. 'In future an idea of the Christ will live in human hearts which in its grandeur cannot be compared with anything that humanity has ever known':[3] these words will become the highest ideal of the new knowledge of the kings.

This means that every person today who is endeavouring to come to a real experience of the Sophia must tread the path of modern spiritual science or Anthroposophy, which enables him to recognise that the Christ Being has been objectively present since the Mystery of Golgotha both in outer nature and in the depths of the human soul, or, which is the same thing, follow the path leading to uniting in himself the qualities of the shepherds and the kings in the new form which is in accordance with modern consciousness.

⋆

An epistemological foundation for such a union can be

found in a very early work by Rudolf Steiner—his book *The Philosophy of Freedom*. In this book a scientific characterisation is given of the cognitive process which arises out of the union in human consciousness of two polar elements: the percept coming from without and the concept corresponding to it springing from the depths of the soul. Only where these are fully and harmoniously combined is there a genuine act of knowledge.

It is not difficult to discern in these two main elements of the cognitive process the characteristic features of, on the one hand, the renewed stream of the shepherds, which aspires towards the spiritualisation of the world of percepts, and, on the other, the renewed stream of the Magi, which seeks the spiritualisation of the world of concepts.

Only on the basis of their real and full union is there a possibility not only for true knowledge in the strictest, scientific sense of this word but also for what proceeds from it, namely, truly *free* human action, which Rudolf Steiner characterises in his book as action that has 'moral imagination' as its foundation. Thus only deeds that are wrought out of 'moral imagination', in which the impulses of the head and the heart are always harmoniously united, are capable of engendering true *goodness* in the world as the highest fruit of the merging of the renewed streams of the shepherds and the kings.

The concluding lines of the fourth part of the Foundation Stone Meditation similarly refer to this higher goal of the union of these streams:

That good may become
What we from our hearts would found,
What we from our heads would direct,
In conscious
Willing.

These lines speak of the need to unite in truly moral (good) deeds the *conscious purpose* associated with them that is intuitively grasped in thinking and the power of love which—as the central power of the heart—lies at their *foundation* as the true source of motivation.

Between these two spiritual pillars of the anthroposophical movement—the *Philosophy of Freedom* and the Christmas Conference, with the Foundation Stone Meditation at its focal point—we have in Rudolf Steiner's spiritual-scientific legacy one particular statement which characterises the two most important tasks of the modern fifth post-Atlantean cultural epoch, or the epoch of the consciousness soul, tasks in which it is not difficult to perceive the present tasks of the transformed streams of the shepherds and the kings.

Thus in the lecture of 14 October 1916[4] Rudolf Steiner spoke of two main elements which must be especially developed amongst mankind over the course of the modern consciousness soul epoch, namely: the phenomenological study of nature and living in free imaginations. We find both of these capacities in the creative work of Goethe. In his scientific studies he laid the foundation for a phenomenological approach to nature, while in the *Fairy Tale of the Green Snake and the*

Beautiful Lily, though even more in the second part of *Faust*, his capacity for living in the world of free imaginations appeared in a full and artistically perfected form.

So Rudolf Steiner was able to build directly on Goethe's achievements, on the one hand by continuing his phenomenological method not only in the realm of sense-perceptible nature—thus laying the foundation of Goetheanism as a new scientific trend of modern times—but also by extending this method to the phenomena of supersensible nature. On the other hand Rudolf Steiner also carried further Goethe's achievements as regards living in free imaginations, by transforming them into a higher faculty of objective knowledge of the spiritual world. For this reason, his first esoteric lecture, the content of which was derived directly from the spiritual world, was given on Michaelmas Day 1900 about the substance of Goethe's *Fairy Tale*.

In this way Rudolf Steiner accomplished on an initiatory level what must be regarded as the most important cultural task of the present epoch, namely, the development and at the same time the uniting within oneself of the capacities for a phenomenological knowledge of nature and for living in free imaginations. As has already been said, it is not difficult to see in these two capacities the chief qualities which the transformed shepherds and the transformed kings need to develop: in the case of the former, this means the phenomenological study of nature, and of the latter, living in free imaginations. For in modern man it is essential that both these two qualities are united.

As we have seen, the supersensible forces of the Sophia are active wherever such a union takes place. Hence they shine through both *The Philosophy of Freedom* and the Christmas Conference of 1923. Their presence in Goethe's creative work was expressed in the famous hymn dedicated to her, with which the great poet concluded his *Faust*. From the lips of the 'mystic choir' there rings forth the praise of the heavenly Sophia, the 'Eternal Feminine':

All that is transient
Is but a parable;
All insufficiency
Here finds fulfilment;
What is ineffable
Here becomes deed;
The Eternal Feminine
Leads us upwards and on.

The need to unite the new faculties of the shepherds and the kings in modern times has a direct relationship with the most important *supersensible* event of our age, the appearance of Christ in etheric form. The whole of mankind must prepare today for the new revelation of Christ from the spiritual world nearest to the Earth. This revelation consists of two clearly distinguishable elements. On the one hand, the imaginative contemplation of the supersensible form of the Christ.

This brings man a new knowledge of His cosmic being and of His relationship with the whole of earthly evolution. On the other hand, the supersensible perception of His voice, which awakens new moral forces in the soul.

One can prepare oneself to perceive both elements of the etheric revelation of the Christ by consciously developing in one's inner being the renewed faculties of the kings and the shepherds. Thus developing the faculties of the kings can lead to a beholding of the etheric countenance of Christ, and developing the faculties of the shepherds can lead to a perceiving of His spiritual word, with whose help He will be able to give a completely new orientation to man's inner life and, in addition, to his social relationships.

As we have seen, the development and union within the soul of *both* kinds of faculties is the result of the working of the supersensible forces of the Sophia in the soul. In this sense the quest for her—which is one of the most important tasks of the Anthroposophical Society—is none other than the conscious development of the new faculties of the shepherds and the Magi. For to the extent that they ripen within the soul, the Sophia herself begins to be present and to work within it, that being who leads man (anthropos) in our time to a conscious experience of the etheric Christ.

In other words, in our time it is *Anthroposophy* which, as the modern synthesis of both paths, the paths of the kings and the shepherds, or—which is the same thing—

the northern and southern mystery streams,* is the representative of the Sophia in the epoch of the consciousness soul. Furthermore, it is simply impossible to discover the Sophia forces without it. And modern mankind needs these Sophia forces as it needs nothing else, for only they can enable it to meet the etheric Christ *consciously*, that is, without sleeping through this central event of our time.

With this the central task of Anthroposophy in the present epoch stands before us: giving the Sophia forces to all human beings of good will, for only with their help can the etheric Christ be found and experienced. In this sense we can understand the following words of Rudolf Steiner, which shall bring this essay to a close: 'Christ will reappear in His spiritual form in the course of the twentieth century not through some outer event but through human beings finding that power which is represented by the holy Sophia.'

★

---

*In the lecture of 19 December 1910 (GA 124), Rudolf Steiner spoke of how the most important trial in the northern mysteries was the meeting with the Great Guardian, while in the southern mysteries it was with the Lesser Guardian. The anthroposophical path of pupilship involves an encounter with both Guardians, which testifies to the union of both paths in the new Christian mysteries as a direct consequence of the Mystery of Golgotha. (Regarding the meeting with the Great and Lesser Guardians of the Threshold, see Rudolf Steiner's books *Knowledge of the Higher Worlds: How is it Achieved?* and *An Outline of Occult Science*.)

Just as the great initiates of humanity took part in the preparation for the physical appearance of the Christ at the Turning Point of Time, so has His supersensible (etheric) appearance in our time been prepared in the higher worlds by spiritual beings. These will be spoken of further in the next essay.

THREE

The Path to a Spiritual Experience of Christ The Appearance of Christ in Etheric Form and the Essential Nature of the Foundation Stone of the Christmas Conference[1]

According to Rudolf Steiner's spiritual-scientific research, one of the most important events of modern times is the fact that the whole of humanity crossed the threshold of the spiritual world in the second half of the nineteenth century.[2] Since then the problem of the threshold has become the central question of the modern age—even though people know little about it, because the crossing of the threshold has initially remained completely unconscious. However, many contemporary events can be understood only out of a knowledge of this underlying fact. Hence, it follows that bringing processes which are now taking place in unconscious regions of the soul into clear, waking consciousness is a task of the utmost importance for our time. Herein also lies the principal task of Anthroposophy. For Anthroposophy seeks above all to bring man to a full consciousness of those processes which have been working unconsciously in his soul life since mankind crossed the threshold of the spiritual world.

Of all the various events of the higher worlds with which man is directly connected, the most important for his future evolution is without doubt the new revelation of Christ in an etheric form or the Second Coming of Christ.[3]

If one searches for the cause of this new appearance of Christ in the twentieth century from a spiritual-scientific point of view, one is brought face to face with another mighty event which Rudolf Steiner describes in his lectures as a kind of repetition of the Mystery of Golgotha in the second half of the nineteenth century, though this time not in the physical but in the spiritual world, in that region which directly borders on the world of human beings.[4] It is significant that on several occasions Rudolf Steiner compares this supersensible Mystery of Golgotha with its historical counterpart, which took place on Earth at the Turning Point of Time. This comparison gives rise to the central question of the considerations that follow.

The historical Mystery of Golgotha, as an earthly event, took place two thousand years ago in Palestine. However, an *understanding* of this central mystery was not given out of earthly powers but came at that time from the spiritual world. Thus on the one hand we have an *earthly* event of a cosmic nature, and, on the other, the understanding of this event comes directly from the *supersensible* world. In Christian tradition, this outpouring of higher knowledge about the Mystery of Golgotha and the earthly life of Christ to His first disciples is called Pentecost.

The second or 'little' Mystery of Golgotha came about in the spiritual world. So it is justifiable to ask with regard to it whether it is possible to find an event in our century which could be indicated as being a kind of *renewed*

Pentecost. In other words, can we find an event in the twentieth century which is able to lead us to a real knowledge of the *repetition* of the Mystery of Golgotha in the higher worlds and also to an experience of the etheric advent of Christ which followed it, in the same way that Pentecost at the Turning Point of Time endowed Christ's most intimate disciples with an understanding of the earthly Mystery of Golgotha? But as the repetition of the Mystery of Golgotha took place not on Earth but in the spiritual world, we must, in accordance with the law of reflection, seek the renewed Pentecost on the physical plane. Is it possible to discern a comparable event in our century?

The present essay is devoted to answering this question. For this, however, it is first necessary to consider Christ's reappearance in an etheric form. In the present context this will have to be done from a quite particular standpoint, namely, by asking oneself which spiritual beings were above all taking part in this central spiritual event of our century by helping and serving it.

★

If one brings everything that Rudolf Steiner ever said about this theme together, one may conclude that there are *three* spiritual beings who participated—and still participate—in this event in a quite particular way. The nature, distinctive qualities and manner of their participation must now be considered in further detail.

The first of the three beings is familiar from many

descriptions by Rudolf Steiner. This is the paradisal, sister-soul of the first man, Adam, who in contrast to him was not subject to the Fall but remained in the spiritual worlds and did not for the time being descend to Earth in a physical body.[5] This soul was protected from the general destiny of humanity by high spiritual beings, and it became the guardian of the heavenly archetype of man in the cosmic spheres. As a spiritual being, this heavenly soul kept out of contact with the Earth over long epochs of time, and merely associated with chosen initiates in the ancient mysteries.

Only once did it appear to humanity in a more direct way, although this revelation was still not an actual incarnation.* In the great proclamation of Krishna, as described in the Bhagavad-Gita, it sent its spiritual light down to earthly humanity for the first time and let its heavenly wisdom ray forth beyond the twilight of the mystery-temples hidden from the great majority of human beings.[6]

However, this paradisal soul was by no means inactive in the spiritual world. On the contrary, in three so-called pre-earthly or cosmic deeds (Rudolf Steiner also calls them preparatory stages of the Mystery of Golgotha) it became the saviour of earthly humanity. On three occasions it sacrificed itself to the Christ in the higher

---

*Rudolf Steiner calls this appearance of the Nathan Soul to humanity a kind of 'vicarious incarnation'. See GA 142, 1 January 1913.

worlds—thereby becoming the bearer of His high Sun Being—in order to divert three great dangers from earthly humanity and at the same time to give it the strength necessary for further evolution. A detailed description of these three cosmic sacrifices can be found in many of Rudolf Steiner's lectures.[7] For present purposes the most important aspect of these sacrificial deeds is that through them the paradisal soul was able to become the ideal of all pre-Christian mysteries, that is to say, the archetypal picture of that higher stage of initiation which in the ancient mysteries was called the stage of 'Christ bearer' or 'Christophorus'.[8] This stage of initiation consisted, in a sense, of the neophyte who had reached it clairvoyantly perceiving the three cosmic deeds of the paradisal soul and at the same time also experiencing them as the successive stages of the divine Christ Being's approach to the Earth.

Only at the Turning Point of Time did this paradisal soul physically incarnate for the first time on the Earth. It was born as Jesus of Nazareth, who was descended from the *Nathan* line of the Hebrew people and whose genealogy is given in St. Luke's Gospel (which is why it is also called the Nathan soul in spiritual-scientific literature).[9] Then at the age of thirty, as a result of the Baptism in the Jordan enacted by John the Baptist, Jesus of Nazareth not only became the bearer of the Christ but was the first and only human being on the Earth to *receive* the Sun Being of Christ right into his physical body. This means that henceforth this paradisal or Nathan soul became an archetype for all human beings of the highest stage of initiation which can be attained in the *new Christian mysteries*. This stage can be called that of being a 'Christ-receiver'. In his lectures Rudolf Steiner clearly distinguishes the tasks of the Nathan soul in the old and new mysteries.[10]

After the Mystery of Golgotha, that is, after the death and Resurrection of Christ in the earthly sheaths of Jesus of Nazareth, the Nathan soul remained united with the Christ Being in the spiritual worlds. Rudolf Steiner says in this connection that after the Mystery of Golgotha the Christ took the Nathan soul 'as His soul [astral] sheath, *through which He then continued to work.*'[11] And at the beginning of the same lecture Rudolf Steiner speaks about the Apostle Paul's clairvoyant experience on the way to Damascus: 'When Paul experiences the revelation before Damascus, it is the Christ who appears to him. But the radiant light in which Christ is clothed is Krishna',[12] that is, the Nathan soul. In other words, it was this soul who appeared to Paul in his vision as the bearer of the fullness of the cosmic Christ consciousness in the blinding streams of radiant astral light, like a mighty aura surrounding the spiritual form of the Risen One.

Because of its very particular relationship with Christ, the Nathan soul also directly participates in His etheric advent in our time. We find a testimony of this in Rudolf Steiner's first mystery-drama, *The Portal of Initiation.*[13] In it there is a scene where Theodora, a seeress, beholds the Christ in etheric form and proclaims this to the people around her. Her wonderful monologue consists—if one reads it carefully—of two parts. In the first part the words come from the etheric Christ Himself. In Theodora's vision He appears as an imaginative form and addresses her in the first person with the words: 'I am', which is in reality His esoteric name, as the God of the human 'I'. The second part of the monologue bears a completely different character (in order to emphasise this more strongly, Rudolf Steiner separates it from the first part by means of a dash). In this second part Theodora describes how a human being appears to her who comes before her clairvoyant gaze out of the radiance or aura of light surrounding the sublime imaginative form of Christ. This human being then addresses her as the direct witness of the etheric Christ, speaking of Him in the third person. It appears to Theodora beside the etheric Christ as a light-filled angel-like being. This being is the Nathan soul, who in our time is a direct participant in the Second Coming.

Thus we are concerned here with two supersensible experiences: one is the experience of Paul and the other the experience of Theodora as portrayed in Rudolf Steiner's mystery-drama. Between them, however, it is not difficult to sense a significant difference. The event which overwhelmed Paul at the gates of Damascus had a mighty, tempestuous character. In the Acts of the Apostles it is described how Paul fell to the ground, went blind and was unable to speak for many days. His whole inner being had been deeply shaken.[14]

A completely different mood fills Theodora's vision. Here there is nothing frightening or stormy. On the contrary, this is a spiritual experience that is full of peace and calm, bathed in a quiet atmosphere of love and gentleness. The difference in the quality of light in the two experiences is especially marked. Paul beholds a mighty cosmic light; through the Nathan soul he experiences the appearance of the *astral* light of the universe itself. In contrast to this, Theodora beholds something altogether different; she contemplates a calm and gentle light. This is the *etheric* light, which is much closer to the earthly sphere than the astral light.*

In order better to understand the difference between these two qualities of light, let us now consider at greater length the event which took place in the spiritual world in the second half of the nineteenth century, referred to by Rudolf Steiner as the repetition of the Mystery of Golgotha. In the lecture of 2 May 1913 he says that in the nineteenth century mankind had attained the highest point in the development of materialism.[15] At that time a number of materialistically inclined individuals, who in

---

* This metamorphosis of the astral light into the etheric light has its foundation in that the four ethers—the warmth, light, chemical and life ethers—are at the same time the reflections (on the level of the etheric) of the four principal planes of world existence. The warmth ether reflects the processes of the physical plane, the *light ether* those of the *astral plane*, the chemical ether reflects processes which have their origin on lower Devachan, and the life ether those originating on higher Devachan.

their lives had thought, felt and acted materialistically, entered after their death into the sphere immediately bordering upon the Earth. As a result the spiritual darkness issuing from them—for materialism spreads darkness in the spiritual world—was so immense that they managed to extinguish the astral light which Paul still beheld in its full radiance, that is, that light wherein lived the cosmic consciousness of Christ, concentrated in the Nathan soul. This destruction of the consciousness of Christ in the Nathan soul is in reality His second crucifixion, though this time not in the physical but in the spiritual world. However, in a manner similar to what happened in the great Mystery of Golgotha, after the destruction of the Christ-consciousness of the Nathan soul there now followed its resurrection through the Sun Spirit of Christ, which continued to work within it. But whereas in the great Mystery of Golgotha the death and Resurrection took place on the level of *being*, now they were repeated on the level of *consciousness*. Moreover, the resurrection came about not in the cosmic sphere of the astral light but at a stage closer to mankind—in the etheric world directly adjoining the earthly domain.[16] Thus through this sacrificial deed of Christ—His death and new resurrection in the Nathan soul—the possibility was created in human evolution for the development of a completely new faculty—the faculty of *a thinking* that is *purely spiritual*. As a result of the supersensible event referred to, the possibility arose on Earth for the living spiritual thinking which appears in our time in the living, spirit-filled thought-forms of modern spiritual science.

Since that time the spiritualised thoughts of human beings, thoughts which are no longer based solely on the activity of the physical brain, have been constantly raying forth into the etheric surroundings of the Earth and can be perceived there by spiritual beings, and also by human beings who are endowed with clairvoyant faculties, to whom the following picture is revealed.

In the modern materialistic epoch the earthly sphere appears to the beings of the higher hierarchies from their heavenly realms as a deep, black abyss, like a night sky devoid of stars. But when here and there people endeavour to understand the spiritual thoughts of Anthroposophy and think them with sufficient intensity, so that in the process of such thinking they are fully able to free themselves from a connection with the physical brain, such spiritualised thoughts begin to shine and radiate from below upwards, from the dark abyss of the Earth into the heavenly realms of the spirit, thus becoming visible to the hierarchies. A new spiritual heaven, full of radiant stars, then appears from below, from the darkness of the earthly sphere.

Such an arising of a new heaven is also a completely new experience for the highest hierarchies. For in the present world-cycle they need the light of the spiritualised thoughts of human beings in order to guide the further evolution of mankind in the right way.

Out of such light-filled, spiritualised thoughts, the Nathan soul then weaves a new, radiant aura for the etheric Christ in that spiritual world which directly borders upon the earthly world. This new radiant aura is the source of that gentle, quietly shining etheric light which Theodora beholds around the imaginative form of Christ. In the rays of this light the Nathan soul itself is revealed to her, as a radiant angel-like being with a human countenance.

From this it becomes understandable that in the Second Coming of Christ the Nathan soul works in a twofold way: macrocosmically and microcosmically. In the macrocosm it is in our time weaving an aura filled with spiritual light for the etheric Christ out of all the spiritual thoughts of human beings. And in the microcosm it is awakening a new capacity of spiritual thinking amongst mankind, a capacity of freeing oneself from the fetters of the physical brain and dwelling in the living thoughts of Anthroposophy.

★

The second spiritual being directly associated with the new advent of Christ is Vidar. He is the only one who survives the twilight of the ancient Gods, and finds the path to the spiritual Sun of Christianity rising over the Earth. Rudolf Steiner speaks at some length about Vidar's relationship with the etheric Christ and his task in the epoch of the Second Coming in the concluding lecture of the cycle *The Mission of the Individual Folk Souls in Relation to Teutonic Mythology*.

In this lecture he unfolds for the first time the mystery

that in our time the task of Vidar is the creation of the etheric form or countenance in which the Christ can appear spiritually to mankind: 'But this other power is known to the mythology of the Germanic North. It knows that this exists. It knows that the etheric countenance exists in which what we shall see as the etheric form of Christ is to be embodied.'[17]

How can this creative activity of Vidar in the higher worlds be understood? A comparison will make this somewhat clearer. When a human soul is in the spiritual world preparing to incarnate again on the Earth, shortly before physical birth it comes to what in earthly language might be described as the shore of the endless sea of the universal ether. It is now necessary for the soul to form its own etheric body out of this cosmic sea. For this it must as it were separate out a certain part of it, condense it and individualise it through its spiritual power, in order then to form from this its own etheric body; and it must do this strictly in accordance with its personal karma, so that this body may become the bearer of its personal dispositions and capacities.

This process can be explained through the following image. If someone here in the earthly world stands on the bank of a river and wants to bring home some water, this will be possible only if he has brought a bucket, pitcher or some other vessel with him. At any rate, a vessel of some kind is necessary in order to fetch water. Such a vessel may have various forms according to choice, but in every case the water poured into it immediately takes its form.

This is the remarkable quality of water—it is always selfless. But what can serve the soul in the spiritual world as such a 'vessel', as that form-creating power with whose help it will be able to form its etheric body out of the endless sea of the world ether (for there are, of course, no such vessels in the spiritual world)? The power which the human soul needs here is the *power of imagination.* With this magical power, which at the present stage of its development the soul still receives from the higher hierarchies in the spiritual worlds, it is able to separate out—as though with a living net—part of the world ether from the general sea of the creative life substance of the cosmos and then individualise it so that a new etheric body can be formed out of it.

Something similar, though at an incomparably higher level, is accomplished by Vidar. As a hierarchic being, he creates through the power of his cosmic imaginations—and out of the purest and highest kinds of ether, those of life and sound[18]—the new etheric form or supersensible sheath for the Christ Himself, in which He will appear to humanity from the twentieth century onwards.

In our time, however, Vidar does not only work in the macrocosm. He also works within man. In the lecture referred to from the cycle on the Folk-Souls, Rudolf Steiner also describes this special task of Vidar in human evolution. There he says that in the present epoch Vidar will 'banish from human souls all the relics of the chaotic, old forces of [atavistic] clairvoyance [inspired by the Fenris Wolf] which would lead man into confusion', and at the same time he will 'awaken in the human breast, in the human soul, the new clairvoyance that is gradually unfolding'. Later in the same lecture, Rudolf Steiner characterises this new clairvoyance as 'irradiated by the light of knowledge and reason'. And so it follows from what has been said that in our time Vidar is that hierarchic spirit who wants to lead mankind to a completely new clairvoyance, to a conscious life in true objective imaginations, through which alone the etheric Christ can be rightly perceived in the spiritual world. Thus in the spiritual activity of Vidar associated with the Second Coming, two aspects can again be clearly distinguished: a spiritual-cosmic aspect and an earthly aspect connected with man. In the macrocosm he creates out of the higher kinds of world ether the new countenance, the new imaginative form for the etheric Christ. He also enters into battle with the demonic being of the astral world—the Fenris Wolf, the inspirer of the dark, atavistic clairvoyance that causes people to be possessed by it. In the microcosm Vidar seeks to awaken in each human individual the capacity of living in conscious imaginations, towards which Anthroposophy indicates a path today. For only such imaginations can lead us to a conscious beholding of the etheric Christ in the spiritual world nearest to the Earth.

★

The third spiritual being who directly participates in the Second Coming of Christ is the ruling Time-Spirit of our epoch, Michael, the great inspirer of modern spiritual science or Anthroposophy.[19] Rudolf Steiner describes the particular relationship of Michael to the appearance of the etheric Christ in the following words: 'This event of the appearance of Christ, as Theodora has indicated it, can only come about if Michael's rulership is extended more and more widely.* This process is for the time being confined to the spiritual world. Michael is battling on the plane which borders upon our world for the coming of Christ.'[20]

For a real understanding of these words of the spirit-researcher of modern times, it is necessary to consider one further important process which is taking place now in the supersensible words. It consists of the following. The materialism that is now so universal has a particularly harmful influence on the human etheric body in the modern epoch. Its occult influence is expressed through man's etheric body becoming ever more rigid and hard as a result of the influence of materialistic thoughts, feelings and will impulses. Rudolf Steiner characterises the condition of such life-bodies as 'wooden'. Such life-bodies dissolve only with great difficulty in the etheric world

---

* These words clearly show that the *whole* of Rudolf Steiner's spiritual-scientific activity, especially during the last years of his life, when he rarely spoke of the etheric advent of Christ but was dedicating all his forces to 'Michael's rulership' being 'extended more and more widely' amongst mankind, must be understood as being a thorough preparation for the supersensible appearance of Christ in our century.

after the death of their bearers. It is as though the spiritual world does not want to receive these 'wooden' life bodies of materialists. They are therefore doomed to an unnaturally long period in the supersensible sphere bordering upon the Earth, where they become the prey of Ahrimanic beings and are made use of by them in their battle against the etheric advent of Christ.[21]

According to Rudolf Steiner's spiritual-scientific observations, the Ahrimanic beings are trying to create something like a 'distorting mirror' in the spiritual world out of these hardened etheric bodies, which would show mankind a distorted image of Christ. With this they want to bring a false imagination of the etheric Christ into the world, so that humanity perceives not the true but a false, distorted image of Him.[22]

Michael, as the ruling spirit of the modern epoch, wages his battle against these hardened and demonically possessed etheric bodies by trying to destroy this distorting mirror. In Rudolf Steiner's words, he battles in the higher worlds 'for the purity of the spiritual horizon'[23] on which the etheric Christ is to appear from our time onwards.

How can we help Michael in his hard struggle against the demonically possessed etheric bodies? In the first place, we must prepare our own etheric bodies in such a way that their forces may help Michael after our death in his fulfilment of this task. And this is possible only if modern spiritual science—as the gift of Michael—is taken up by anthroposophists not only in their astral bodies but at the much deeper level of their etheric bodies.

This means that Anthroposophy must not only live in our thinking as some sort of new teaching but influence our whole character, all our habits and inner inclinations, including our social relationships. In other words, only if spiritual science becomes as vitally necessary for us as the circulation of the blood, or as the air we breathe, will it really be able to permeate our etheric bodies and gradually transform them in such a way that their forces can work to Michael's advantage. And then after our death we shall ourselves be honoured with taking part in his supersensible battle.

A further indication in the same direction can be found in the lecture-cycle *Michaelmas and the Soul-Forces of Man.*[24] In this cycle Rudolf Steiner describes how in our Michaelic age the imagination of Michael battling against the dragon has become of such immense significance in the spiritual worlds that a reflection of this event can be found in the etheric body of every human individual incarnated on the Earth, even though for the majority of people today this help of Michael remains unconscious. However, if we work intensively with Anthroposophy, this reflection can not only be fully part of our conscious lives but also be strengthened to the extent that it eventually has a direct influence on the etheric forces of our hearts. This is a new way in which earthly man can collaborate with Michael, a path which leads to a conscious penetration of the great mystery of the etheric heart.

Rudolf Steiner unfolds this mystery in the lecture *The Etherisation of the Blood. The Entry of the Etheric Christ into Earthly Evolution.*[25] There he describes how in every earthly human being a spiritual-etheric stream is constantly rising from the heart to the head. However, since the Mystery of Golgotha a further stream has united with this stream of etherised human blood—the stream of the etherised blood of the Christ Himself. Both these streams are visible to the modern Christian initiate. But an ordinary person knows nothing about them. For such a person both streams flow parallel without touching one another. Only when they have been united in one single stream will—according to Rudolf Steiner—a conscious perception of the etheric Christ be achieved.

The most important condition for the union of these two streams is the complete purification of the spiritual region of the heart that is associated with driving from it all the forces of the Ahrimanic dragon, which, as the result of materialism and its various manifestations in human life, have been entering right into it for the last three or four centuries. In this connection, if we look upon modern materialistic civilisation one has to state: the dragon has in our time already won mastery over the etheric hearts of countless people. It is therefore necessary to drive it out, something which is possible only through the strengthening of the reflection of the cosmic imagination of Michael in the life-body of man.

The result of inner work in this direction will be the gradual union of man's own will with the cosmic intentions of Michael with respect to contemporary humanity. For today Michael is, in Rudolf Steiner's words, himself seeking a path to man. He would wish to reach through the head of man to his heart, in order to find there for himself a new field of activity for the sake of the future evolution of the Earth.[26]

Thus we see that Michael is working today in two different directions. In the macrocosm he purifies the spiritual sphere bordering upon the Earth for the etheric Christ. While microcosmically he endeavours to give every human being a new power capable of penetrating to his etheric heart, in order to free him from the might of the Ahrimanic dragon.

★

In conclusion, we must consider the central figure of the Second Coming—the Christ Being Himself. Similarly, in His activity within earthly evolution two different trends can be discerned.

First and foremost, the Christ appears in the macrocosm as the great Bearer of universal love. Since the time of His union with the Earth through the Mystery of Golgotha, He has striven gradually to transform it into a new moral Sun, and to turn the old cosmos of wisdom and law into a future cosmos of freedom and love.[27] Microcosmically, the Christ has worked since the Mystery of Golgotha as described above, by being immutably present in each earthly human being through the stream of His etherised blood, which is the bearer of the substance of universal love in the being of man.

★

We can now gather together all the aspects of the re-appearance of Christ that have been mentioned, in order to arrive at a single image of this central spiritual event of our time, placing before ourselves the *universal* and at the same time the *human* imagination of His Second Coming. We shall first consider the human aspect of this imagination, which is associated with the etheric body.

In every human being since the Mystery of Golgotha there has flowed the etheric blood of Christ, the bearer of the sacrificial *substance of love*, constantly streaming upwards from the heart to the head. However, ordinary consciousness knows nothing of this, as the etherised blood simply passes through such a person and then unites with the spiritual world surrounding him. For this reason we need the new *imaginations* which Vidar can give us today through spiritual science, in order that we may really experience the stream of the etheric blood of Christ in our own etheric body. These imaginations will then become for us a kind of supersensible vessel, or spiritual chalice, in which we will be able to gather this flowing etheric substance of the love of Christ and, through this, experience it. We then need the *light of spiritual thoughts*, the light of the new consciousness of Christ which the Nathan soul has kindled in human beings through its fifth sacrificial deed in the evolution of mankind.[28] With this light of spiritualised thoughts one is then able to illumine the imagination of the chalice, in order to raise it from heart to head and thus fully bring this process into one's consciousness.

All this can, however, become a reality in one's etheric body only if a mighty image appears within it, as though on the horizon of the process which is being described—the reflection of the Spirit of Michael conquering the dragon in the human heart and casting it down to the realm of the limbs and metabolic system.[29]

This is the true experience of the mysteries of the Holy Grail as renewed out of the Michaelic Time-Spirit.

If this inner process, which can in our time be experienced by each human individual, is so strengthened through working with Anthroposophy that it gradually enters into one's consciousness, one will sooner or later be able to perceive in the spiritual world what is manifested there as the great *macrocosmic archetype* of the microcosmic mystery of one's etheric heart that has been described above.

Then the etheric Christ Himself will appear before one's now clairvoyant gaze, as the divine Bearer of the *substance of cosmic love*.* He will approach one from the depths of the spiritual world in the new *imaginative form*

---

* The etheric body is as regards its inner nature woven out of love, and can therefore be called a 'body of love' (Rudolf Steiner, lecture of 2 December 1911 in Nuremberg). The etheric body of the Christ is a revelation of cosmic love.

which Vidar has fashioned for Him out of the purest forces of the life and sound ethers, surrounded by the light-filled and rainbow-spangled aura woven for Him by the Nathan soul out of all the spiritual human thoughts which have been received by the hierarchies in the spiritual world and are permeated by their *universal thoughts*. And on the horizon of this majestic manifestation the mighty *Spirit* of Michael will be present, waging his battle with the Ahrimanic demons who oppose the etheric advent and who make use of the hardened etheric bodies of materialistically inclined human beings.[30]

★

If one carefully considers this cosmic and at the same time human imagination of the etheric Christ, one may observe that it contains all the essential elements out of which Rudolf Steiner created the *Foundation Stone* of the General Anthroposophical Society on 25 December 1923 at the Christmas Conference, to which he gave the supersensible form of a double dodecahedron: the dodecahedron of the world and of man.★ Rudolf Steiner

---

★ The Foundation Stone was given the form of a dodecahedron, which consists of twelve pentagrams pointing in all directions of space. The pentagram is the esoteric symbol of a perfect human being. But in the dodecahedron it is united with the whole twelvefold (zodiacal) cosmos. The esoteric tradition of the Grail speaks of how in order to find its resting-place (the Grail Castle) it is necessary to journey through a wild, impenetrable forest for a distance of sixty miles. Sixty is a reference to the mystery of the dodecahedron (5 times 12).

characterises this double Foundation Stone as follows: 'This is that Foundation Stone, which has received its substance from universal love and human love, its figurative quality and form from universal imagination and human imagination, and its brilliant radiance from universal thoughts and human thoughts, so that every time when we remember this moment its warming, inspiring light can shine towards our deeds, our thoughts, our feelings and our will.'[31]

Somewhat later in the same address Rudolf Steiner spoke about it in the following words, which were directly addressed to those taking part in the Christmas Conference: 'Listen to these words [of the Foundation Stone Meditation], my dear friends, and may this resound in your hearts! Then will you found a true community of human beings for *Anthroposophia*, and bring the *spirit* that rules in the shining light of thoughts around the dodecahedral stone of love out into the world, bring it wherever it should give light and warmth for the evolution of human souls, for the evolution of the world.'

Thus at the Christmas Conference the Foundation Stone of the General Anthroposophical Society was formed out of the substance of universal and human love, that is, out of the substance of the Christ as it has been working since the Mystery of Golgotha both in the world and in man. Its form was created out of universal and human imaginations with their living figurative quality, the fruit of the activity of Vidar in the spiritual cosmos and in man. It was then engirdled by the universal and human thoughts which are the result of the spiritual activity of the Nathan soul in the cosmos and in man's being. And finally, it was illumined by the presence of the Spirit who, as the Spirit of our Michaelic age, himself appeared 'in the shining light of thoughts around the dodecahedral stone of love', that is, in the shining light of the redeemed cosmic intelligence,[32] in order to work together with mankind in the new epoch of freedom 'for the evolution of human souls, for the evolution of the world'.

So the Foundation Stone is composed of three parts: the substance of love, which affords a real experience of Christ through a spiritual communion with His Being; the imaginations filled with cosmic life, through which the Christ can be consciously perceived in His etheric advent in our time; and the radiant light of spiritualised thoughts, through which it becomes possible for the first time for man to gain a true knowledge of Christ. And what crowns it all is the appearance of the Spirit in this light of thoughts, in the light of the redeemed intelligence of Michael shining around the imagination of the Foundation Stone.

This individually active Spirit—who through his very nature can only be received by man individually and in full freedom into his soul, into his heart—is at the same time a Spirit who unites and thereby creates a new human community, leading those who are inwardly working with the Foundation Stone Meditation to 'a true community of human beings for Anthroposophia'. This is what must increasingly become established on the basis of the Christmas Conference of the General Anthroposophical Society: a community of people filled and inspired by this individually apprehensible and at the same time socially active Spirit who unites human beings, in order that on its foundation there may begin to be established a new, *purely spiritual brotherhood* in human evolution.

★

It follows from what has been said that the Foundation Stone of the Christmas Conference of 1923–1924 is in its esoteric essence a real *organ of perception* for the knowledge and experience of the etheric Christ. From this it becomes understandable why this Foundation Stone, also called by Rudolf Steiner the 'dodecahedral Stone of Love', can be 'laid' or 'implanted into the soil of our hearts'. As what is meant here is the 'soil' of the etheric heart, this means that the Foundation Stone must be implanted in precisely that region of our life-bodies where the twofold etheric mystery described above takes place—the macrocosmic mystery of the etherisation of the blood of Christ and the microcosmic mystery of the etherisation of the blood of man.

Herein also lies the key to the mystery of the *twofold* aspect of the Foundation Stone—because only a pure and spiritualised human love can really comprehend the universal love of Christ. Thus Rudolf Steiner writes in

Anthroposophical Leading Thoughts: 'The event of Golgotha is a free cosmic deed which springs from universal love and is intelligible only by the love in man.'[33] Similarly, the universal imagination of the etheric Christ can become visible only through new, fully conscious human imaginations; and the light of the cosmic intelligence shining around the form of Christ can be apprehended only with the help of fully spiritualised, light-bearing human thoughts. 'Then in our soul's perception we can bring the dodecahedron of man face to face with the dodecahedron of the universe,' said Rudolf Steiner at the Christmas Conference on 25 December.

This double dodecahedron, as a radiant 'Foundation Stone of the imagination', must then be nurtured and fostered in the depths of the human heart, where through its twofold nature it can bring about a gradual union of the two etheric streams, that is, lead those human beings working with it to a perception of the etheric Christ and to a conscious collaboration with Him and with the spiritual beings who serve Him referred to above.

In this sense the Christmas Conference has a relationship not only to the past but also the present and future. For at each moment of our lives, if we do but strive towards this, we can lay the 'Foundation Stone of the imagination' in the soil of our hearts. Then the living substance of the Christmas Conference will become present amongst us as a new supersensible reality blossoming in our hearts and leading into the future. It must, however, be continually borne in mind that this sacramental act of laying the Foundation Stone 'in the soil of our hearts' is not something which can be brought about once and for all but is something which, as a free vow of our unshakeable faithfulness to the living being Anthroposophia, must constantly be renewed in our souls.

If we can but work actively in this direction, we shall be able to perceive from the very nature of the Foundation Stone that, as separate individualities, we are capable of fulfilling only the *human* aspect of it. If we are to add the second, *universal* aspect to the twofold Stone, we need to unite with other human beings who are working in the world out of the same spirit.

Such an awareness of the community-forming impulse springing from the Spirit who appears in the light of the Foundation Stone may help us to understand still more deeply the esoteric essence and spiritual aims of the General Anthroposophical Society founded at the Christmas Conference. Now not merely our heads but also our hearts are able to sense that working only as individuals or in separate groups studying spiritual science is not enough; for the establishing on Earth of a new universally human community is an absolute necessity for the realisation of the universal aspect of the Foundation Stone, and this aim cannot be attained on other paths.

In this sense one can say that at the Christmas Conference a society was founded which sought to be a community of free individualities who, out of *individually* attained knowledge, wish *together* to form on Earth a living human vessel for the etheric Christ and the spiritual beings serving Him to work amongst mankind.

Only a real understanding of this lofty task of the Anthroposophical Society can enable the inner essence of the Christmas Conference to be revealed to us as the spiritual act of laying the foundations for a human community which has the task of becoming the germinal beginnings of a true spiritual community on Earth. Then this Christmas Conference will become for us the most significant earthly event of the twentieth century, which should be understood as a *renewed Pentecost* in the sense of the reversed cultus described by Rudolf Steiner.*[34]

This renewed Pentecost will become for us a conscious path—not only for separate individuals but above all for a new, world-embracing human community—to a supersensible experience, direct perception and deep spiritual understanding of the all-encompassing reality of the Second Coming of Christ.

---

* This renewed Pentecost can also be called 'reversed' in the sense that the original Pentecost at the Turning Point of Time brought the disciples first an understanding of the Mystery of Golgotha and then a real understanding of the earthly life of Christ that had preceded it. (See Rudolf Steiner, lecture of 2 October 1913 in Christiania (Oslo), GA 148.) With respect to it the impulse of the renewed Pentecost of the Christmas Conference manifests the reverse course of events: first it leads to a conscious perception of the appearance of Christ in the etheric body and then from it to the second, supersensible Mystery of Golgotha, as the spiritual source of this event.

If we take all this into consideration, we can now understand in what sense Rudolf Steiner said at the very end of the Christmas Conference, on 1 January 1924: 'This Christmas, this Christmas festival is to be for us not only the beginning of a new year but also the *beginning of a world Turning Point of Time*', that is, the *beginning* of a second or new 'world Turning Point of Time'[35] associated with the appearance of Christ in an etheric body, in the same sense in which the first 'world Turning Point of Time' was associated with the appearance of Christ in a physical body in ancient Palestine.

The Holy Spirit who brought knowledge of the Christ descended at Whitsun to the apostles in tongues of spiritual fire. He revealed himself to them as separate individualities, not overshining them all together but resting on the head of *each* of them separately, though in such a way that they were all filled with the *one* Spirit: 'And there appeared to them tongues as of fire, distributed and resting on *each one* of them, And they were *all* filled with the Holy Spirit' (Acts 2:3–4).* As an act of the highest wisdom the Holy Spirit was sent down at that

---

*We also have the same sequence in the Foundation Stone Meditation, at the beginning of which there is an individual addressing of *each* human soul: 'Soul of man!' and then in the fourth part, beginning from the lines 'At the Turning Point of Time/The *Light of the World-Spirit*/Entered the stream of earthly being', there follow the words 'That good may become/what *we* ...' This transition from individual knowledge to a common enacting of the good is fully in accordance with the Spirit of Whitsun.

moment to their heads in order then to speak forth from their hearts. This happened through the mediation of the etheric stream coming from the macrocosm, which Rudolf Steiner, in his lecture on *The Etherisation of the Blood*, characterises as a stream which flows continuously from the spiritual world to the human head and from thence down in the direction of the heart. Rudolf Steiner also calls it the 'moral-etheric' stream, since through it moral, divine-spiritual forces come to man continuously from the cosmos. It was out of this spiritual source 'from above', in the direction 'from above downwards', that the new community *for human beings* was founded at Pentecost.

From the twentieth century onwards, anthroposophists are now called to renew this event out of the Michaelic Time-Spirit. But this will only happen if they are really able to lay the Foundation Stone of the Christmas Conference in their hearts, in order to establish upon it a new human community which seeks to become a conscious instrument for the work of the etheric Christ—and the hierarchic beings who help Him—amongst mankind. Through this the Anthroposophical Society can become a bridge on the Earth where human beings learn to work together with the Gods, in order with them to serve and help the etheric Christ.

Today, however, this has to take place on a new path, in the spirit of a renewed Pentecost. This is because mankind has entered the epoch of freedom. This new mystery of Pentecost is enacted not only through the outpouring of grace from above downwards but also through the free participation of man, as he lays the Stone of Love in his etheric heart, so that the Spirit who is revealed in the radiant aura of the Stone of Love can rise from the heart up to the head and from thence shine forth into the darkness of the outer world. This 'ascent of the Spirit' comes about through the other stream—already described above—which Rudolf Steiner, in his lecture on *The Etherisation of the Blood*, calls the microcosmic stream of the etherised blood of man, that stream which rises in every human being in a reverse direction, from the heart to the head, and from there out into the spiritual world that surrounds us.

We have a reference to this stream in the fourth, concluding part of the Foundation Stone Meditation, where first the heart is mentioned three times and then the head, which bears out the etheric movement from below upwards, from heart to head. In the lecture referred to Rudolf Steiner calls this ascending stream the 'intellectual' stream, since the Michaelic intelligence dwelling in man is associated with it. And parallel to this stream, likewise ascending from the heart to the head, flows the stream of the etherised blood of Christ;[36] and through man's becoming conscious of this he can redeem the Michaelic intelligence.

We can understand this process of redemption as follows. If, through laying the dodecahedral Stone of Love in its twofold nature in the soil of the etheric heart, a gradual union of these two *ascending* streams into one single stream takes place in the region of the etheric heart, the Michaelic intelligence dwelling in man will then be transformed and spiritualised. As a result, the light of the spiritualised thoughts which, like a radiant aura, surrounds the Stone of Love will—by uniting with the ascending etheric stream—be able to spread out in the direction from the heart to the head, while being transmuted in this movement upwards from light into fire. And as in this process of light becoming fire the Spirit is both present and active, this Spirit will be able to bear on its wings the purified and transformed intelligence of man living in the etheric stream beyond the limits of the human head and directly into the spiritual world. Then in this column of fire, man himself will in his consciousness be able to rise into the higher world together with the transformed and Spirit-imbued intelligence.

Thus out of the Time-Spirit of the present epoch there will be brought about that baptism 'with the Holy Spirit and with fire' of which John the Baptist prophetically spoke at the Turning Point of Time. (Matthew 3:11, Luke 3:16) With this it will become possible for man *consciously* to enter that spiritual sphere where the etheric Christ works today, in order there to become His collaborator and helper for the good of earthly evolution as a whole.

That good may become
What we from our hearts would found
What we from our heads would direct

In conscious
Willing.

★

Having once entered this sphere of universal goodness—which in our time is the true Shambala[37]—out of the forces of the inner, spiritual fire of a renewed Pentecost, we shall be able to experience in it the revelation of Christ for our present time in all its fiery strength: 'Indeed, just as Moses and his followers experienced an anticipation of the future appearance of Christ in the burning bush and the lightning on Sinai, so will the Christ appear to us in the spiritualised fire of the future.'[38] 'And lo, I am with you always, to the end of the earthly age', says Christ. (Matthew 28:20) 'He will appear in spiritual fire to those who have allowed their perception to be illuminated by the event of Golgotha. Human beings will contemplate Him in the spiritual fire.'

In this macrocosmic fire, visible to the soul which has been able to kindle within itself the microcosmic fire of a renewed Pentecost that is related to it, the Christ will be revealed in His ineffable universal majesty, as the God of the human 'I', as the universal 'I am'. Then 'they will see the Son of man coming on the clouds of heaven with power and with great glory.' (Matthew 24:30) From the sources of his spiritual research Rudolf Steiner also speaks of this: 'They [the Christians of the future] will not merely understand the Christ who has passed through death; they will also comprehend the conquering

Christ—resurrected in spiritual fire—of the Apocalypse, who was proclaimed.'

Only out of the modern mysteries of the etheric Christ are we able today to derive the inner forces that we need to withstand all the strengthening forces of evil in the world, and the Foundation Stone of the Good laid by Rudolf Steiner at the foundation of the new human community can become for us the gateway to these mysteries.

Notes

Chapter One (pages 1–105)

1 See GA 152, 2 May 1913.
2 See GA 185, 25 October 1918.
3 Ibid.
4 GA 185, 26 October 1918.
5 GA 145, 29 March 1913.
6 GA 239, 8 June 1924.
7 GA 131, 14 October 1911.
8 GA 266/1, 1 November 1906.
9 GA 107, 22 March 1909.
10 See GA 104, 29 June 1908.
11 See GA 184, 11 & 12 October 1918.
12 See GA 171, 25 September 1916.
13 GA 197, 13 June 1920.
14 GA 174, 22 January 1917.
15 GA 198, 3 April 1920.
16 Ibid.
17 See also S. O. Prokofieff *The Spiritual Origins of Eastern Europe and the Future Mysteries of the Holy Grail*, Temple Lodge Publishing, London 1993.
18 See GA 131, 5 October 1911; GA 197, 30 July & 21 September 1920.
19 See, for example, C. Lindenberg *Die Technik des Bösen. Zur Vorgeschichte und Geschichte des National-Sozialismus*, the chapter entitled 'Ermächtigungsgesetz gegen Konkordat', 3rd edition 1985.

20 See GA 190, 5 April 1919.
21 See GA 186, 1 December 1918.
22 See GA 174, 20 & 22 January 1917.
23 Ga 197, 13 June 1920.
24 GA 346, 12 September 1924.
25 GA 346, 20 September 1924.
26 GA 11 and 13.
27 GA 171, 25 September 1916.
28 Ibid.
29 GA 171, 1 October 1916.
30 GA 171, 25 September 1916.
31 GA 346, 12 September 1924.
32 GA 107, 22 March 1909.
33 Ibid.
34 Ibid.
35 See also GA 104, 30 June 1908.
36 GA 346, 12 September 1924.
37 GA 346, 15 September 1924.
38 GA 346, 17 September 1924.
39 See, for example, A. Schmelzer *Die Menschheitskrise der Gegenwart, 666–1332–1998, Zeitsymptome und Erziehungsaufgaben*, Dornach 1998.
40 GA 198, 3 April 1920.
41 GA 197, 13 June 1920.
42 See in particular GA 193, 27 October & 4 November 1919.
43 See GA 193, 4 November 1919.
44 GA 197, 13 June 1920.
45 GA 202, 25 December 1920.
46 GA 194, 15 December 1919.
47 See GA 97, 30 November 1906.
48 GA 131, 5 October 1911.
49 See GA 177, 26 October 1917.
50 GA 233a, 13 January 1924.

51 GA 185, 2 November 1918.
52 Ibid. See also Note 17.
53 GA 13.
54 GA 10.
55 GA 26, article 'From Nature to Sub-Nature', March 1925.
56 GA 175, 13 March 1917.
57 GA 175, 6 February 1917.
58 GA 260, 25 December 1923.
59 See GA 118, 6 March 1910.
60 GA 260, 26 December 1923.
61 Ibid.
62 See further regarding the spiritual nature of the Foundation Stone in S. O. Prokofieff *Rudolf Steiner and the Founding of the New Mysteries*, Chapter 7, Temple Lodge Publishing, London 1994.
63 GA 260, 25 December 1923.
64 GA 148, 2 October 1913.
65 For further details about the connection between the etheric appearance of Christ and the threefold nature of the Foundation Stone, see S. O. Prokofieff *The Cycle of the Year as a Path of Initiation. An Esoteric Study of the Festivals*, Part XII, 'The Modern Mysteries of the Etheric Christ, Temple Lodge Publishing, London 1995.
66 See GA 120, 27 May 1910.
67 GA 112, 6 July 1909.
68 See GA 13.
69 GA 185, 26 October 1918.
70 See GA 112, 24 June 1909.
71 GA 13.
72 See GA 264, p.218.
73 GA 13.
74 GA 118, 20 February 1910.
75 GA 158, 9 November 1914.

76 GA 266/1, 23 October 1907.
77 GA 130, 18 November 1911.
78 GA 10.
79 GA 26, article of 23 November 1924 'The World Thoughts in the Working of Michael and in the Working of Ahriman'.
80 GA 116, 8 May 1910.
81 GA 182, 16 October 1918.
82 GA 107, 22 March 1909.
83 GA 194, 15 December 1919.
84 GA 200, 30 October 1920.
85 See, for example, GA 266/1, 1 November 1906.
86 See, for example, GA 184, 4 October 1918; GA 203, 11 March 1921.
87 GA 104, 29 June 1908.
88 Ibid.

Chapter Two (pages 107–131)

1 Based on a lecture given in Moscow on 16 May 1998 at the conference 'The Quest of the Sophia in the Present'. A further development of the principal themes touched upon in this essay can be found in the author's book *The Heavenly Sophia and the Being Anthroposophia*, Temple Lodge Publishing, London 1996. Similar allusions—and bibliographical references—to the lectures by Rudolf Steiner used in the present essay can also be found there.

All the quotations from Rudolf Steiner are taken from his lecture cycle *The Search for the New Isis, the Divine Sophia* given from 23 to 26 December 1920 in Basle and Dornach (GA 202).

The original text of the Foundation Stone Meditation is contained in GA 260.

F. W. Zeylmans van Emmichoven's book *Der Grundstein* (1956) was published in English translation in 1963 (*The Foundation Stone*, Rudolf Steiner Press, London). See especially the chapter entitled 'The Pentagram and the Sun of Christ'.

2 GA 15.

3 Ibid.

4 GA 171, 14 October 1916.

Chapter Three (pages 133–168)

1 The present essay is based on a lecture that I originally gave on 30 December 1989 at the Goetheanum in Dornach. It was dedicated to the 66th anniversary of the Christmas Conference (24 December 1923 to 1 January 1924). This lecture was subsequently given in Russia, and also in Germany, Switzerland, England and North America, which I visited at the invitation of the Anthroposophical Societies of these countries.

The reader can find a further development and deepening of the main theme of this essay in my book *The Cycle of the Year as a Path of Initiation, An Esoteric Study of the Christian Festivals* (second edition, Temple Lodge Publishing, London 1995, part XII, 'The Modern Mysteries of the Etheric Christ'). Familiarity with this book will be of significant help in understanding what follows.

2 GA 233a, 12 & 13 January 1924; (see *Rosicrucianism and Modern Initiation*).

3 GA 15, 118, 123, 130, 131, and other lectures.

4 GA 152, 2 & 20 May 1913.

5 GA 114, 142 & 146.

6 Ibid., and GA 146.

7 GA 148, 149, 152; also GA 233a, 21 April 1924.

8 GA 187, 27 December 1918; GA 233a, 21 April 1924, and other lectures.

9 GA 114 and 146.

10 GA 233a, 21 April 1924.

11 GA 142, 1 January 1913. (Author's italics.)

12 See Footnote on p. 138.

13 GA 14, *The Portal of Initiation*, Sc.1. Also Note 84 to Part XII in S. O. Prokofieff *The Cycle of the Year as a Path of Initiation. An Esoteric Study of the Festivals*, Temple Lodge Publishing, London 1995.

14 The Acts of the Apostles, Chapter 9.

15 GA 152, 2 May 1913.

16 For a more detailed description of this process, see S. O. Prokofieff *The Cycle of the Year as a Path of Initiation*, op. cit., Part XII, Chapter 2. Regarding the relationship between the astral and the etheric light, see Note 98 to Part XII.

17 GA 121, 17 June 1910.

18 GA 114, 21 September 1909. In this lecture is described how these two higher kinds of ether were protected by the higher hierarchies from the Fall at the dawn of Earth existence.

19 GA 26; GA 152, 2 May 1913; GA 217, 15 October 1922; GA 237 & 240.

20 GA 158, 9 November 1914.

21 A similar influence upon the etheric body is also exercised by all kinds of modern nationalism, which from an occult point is merely a special form of materialism. See also Note 22.

22 GA 174a, 3 December 1914; see also Note 20.

23 Ibid.

24 GA 223.

25 GA 130, 1 October 1911.

26 GA 26, the articles entitled 'At the Dawn of the Michael Age' and 'The Condition of the Human Soul before the Dawn of the Michael Age', August 1924.

27 GA 13, the chapter entitled 'Present and Future Evolution of the World and of Mankind'.

28 According to spiritual science there are three 'pre-earthly' deeds of Christ through the Nathan soul (see Note 7), followed by the *earthly* Mystery of Golgotha, the central event of earthly evolution. In our time, this is now followed by a new supersensible deed of Christ through the Nathan soul (the fifth). This will in future be followed by a sixth and a seventh (see Notes 4 and 16).

29 See Note 24.

30 For further details about the universal and human imagination of the etheric appearance of Christ, see the book referred to in Note 13.

31 GA 260, also the following quotation in which the italics are the author's.

32 See GA 237 and 240, and also GA 26. In these contexts Rudolf Steiner says that the original task of Michael in our cosmos was the rulership of the cosmic intelligence (or 'reason'), that is, all the creative thoughts of the spiritual hierarchies. After the Mystery of Golgotha Michael sacrificed this heavenly intelligence, so that with its help human beings on Earth could comprehend the divine Christ Being and the entire cosmic-earthly significance of the Mystery of Golgotha which He accomplished. However, once the heavenly intelligence had become earthly, it was to a significant extent taken hold of within man by Ahrimanic powers and in this ahrimanised form served as a foundation for *materialistic* science. In this connection Rudolf Steiner indicates that

among the most important tasks of the present Michaelic epoch (which began in 1879) is the gradual spiritualisation (redemption) of this heavenly intelligence (reason) which has become earthly and its utilisation for a new, spiritual–scientific understanding of the Mystery of Golgotha—the central event of earthly and world evolution—and also of the supersensible appearance of Christ in our time.

33 GA 26, Leading Thought No. 143.

34 GA 257, 27 February & 3 March 1923. In these lectures Rudolf Steiner speaks at length about the spiritual nature of the 'reversed cultus' ('*umgekehrter Kultus*'), in which, pictorially speaking, it is not a case of the Angels descending to human beings, as in a sacramental cultus (religious service), but of human beings gradually ascending in their consciousness to the sphere of the Angels (initiation).

35 See Note 31.

36 See Note 25. Also S. O. Prokofieff *The Cycle of the Year as a Path of Initiation*, op. cit. (Part I, Chapter 1 & 2; Part II, Chapter 3.)

37 Regarding Shambala as the modern domain of the etheric Christ in the spiritual environment of the Earth, see GA 118, 6 & 15 March 1910.

38 GA 109, 11 April 1909. The quotations that follow are from the same source.

List of Works by Rudolf Steiner Referred to in the Present Book

The following list is intended above all to enable the English-speaking reader to discover where—if at all—the books and lectures referred to in the text and notes may be found in English translation. (It is not intended as a comprehensive bibliography.) Where the volume in the German *Gesamtausgabe* series (GA)—the complete edition of Rudolf Steiner's works—is represented by an equivalent publication in English, the title of this is given. Where this is not the case, reference is made to the publications or typescripts where the lectures specified may be found. (Typescript references are to the collection at the library of Rudolf Steiner House, 35 Park Rd., London NW1 6XT.) If the lectures have not been translated, the German title of the GA volume is given.

GA 10 *Knowledge of the Higher Worlds*
11 *Cosmic Memory*
13 *Occult Science—An Outline*
14 *The Four Mystery Plays*
15 *The Spiritual Guidance of Man and Humanity*
26 *Anthroposophical Leading Thoughts*
93 *The Temple Legend*
97 30 November 1906: *The Three Paths of Initiation* (Typescript Z 208)
104 *The Apocalypse of St. John*

107 22 March 1909: *The Deed of Christ and the Opposing Spiritual Powers*

109 11 April 1909: *The Principle of Spiritual Economy*

112 *The Gospel of St. John in Relation to the Other Three Gospels*

114 *The Gospel of St. Luke*

116 *The Christ Impulse and the Development of Ego-Consciousness*

118 6, 15 March 1910 and other lectures: *The Reappearance of Christ in the Etheric*
20 February 1910: *The Sermon on the Mount and the Return of Christ* (Typescript Z 295)

120 *Manifestations of Karma*

121 *The Mission of the Individual Folk Souls in Relation to Teutonic Mythology*

123 *The Gospel of St. Matthew*

124 *Background to the Gospel of St. Mark*

130 18 November 1911: *Esoteric Christianity and the Mission of Christian Rosenkreutz*
1 October 1911: *The Etherisation of the Blood* (also in *The Reappearance of Christ in the Etheric*)
2, 3 December 1911: *Faith, Love, Hope*

131 *From Jesus to Christ*

142 *The Bhagavad-Gita and the Epistles of Paul*

145 *The Effects of Spiritual Development*

146 *The Occult Foundations of the Bhagavad-Gita*

148 *The Fifth Gospel*

149 *Christ and the Spiritual World. The Search for the Holy Grail*

152 2 May 1913: *Occult Science and Occult Development*
20 May 1913: *The Festivals and their Meaning*

7 March 1914: *Pre-Earthly Deeds of Christ*
1 June 1914: *The Four Sacrifices of Christ* and other lectures

157 *Destinies of Individuals and of Nations*

158 9 November 1914: *The Connection of Man with the Elemental World—Finland and the Kalevala* (Typescript Z 144)

171 *Inner Impulses of Human Evolution*

174 *The Karma of Untruthfulness vol. 2*

174a *Mitteleuropa zwischen Ost und West*

175 6 February 1917 and 13 March 1917: *Cosmic and Human Metamorphosis*

177 *The Fall of the Spirits of Darkness*

178 16 November 1917: *Geographic Medicine—the Mystery of the Double*

182 16 October 1918: *How do I find the Christ?*

184 4, 11, 12, October 1918: *Three Streams in the Evolution of Mankind*

185 *From Symptom to Reality in Modern History*

186 1, 7 December 1918: *The Challenge of the Times*

187 *How Can Mankind Find the Christ Again?*

190 *Vergangenheits- und Zukunftsimpulse im sozialen Geschehen*

191 1 November 1919: *Influences of Lucifer and Ahriman. Man's Responsibility for the Earth*

193 27 October 1919: *The Ahrimanic Deception*
4 November 1919: *Influences of Lucifer and Ahriman. Man's Responsibility for the Earth*

194 15 December 1919: *Mysteries of Light, Space and of the Earth.* Also in: *Ideas for a New Europe*

195 *The Cosmic New Year*

197 *Polarities in the Evolution of Mankind*

198 *Heilfaktoren für den sozialen Organismus*
200 *The New Spirituality and the Christ Experience of the Twentieth Century*
202 23–26 December 1920: *The Search for the New Isis, the Divine Sophia*
203 11 March 1921: *The Responsibility of Man for World Evolution through his Spiritual Connection with the Planet Earth and the World of Stars* (Typescript R 62)
217 *The Younger Generation*
223 27 September 1923—1 October 1923: *Michaelmas and the Soul Forces of Man*
233a 12, 13 January 1924: *Rosicrucianism and Modern Initiation*
19, 22 April 1924: *The Easter Festival in the Evolution of the Mysteries*
237 *Karmic Relationships vol. 3*
239 *Karmic Relationships vol. 5*
240 *Karmic Relationships vols. 6 and 8*
257 *Awakening to Community*
260 *The Christmas Conference for the Founding of the General Anthroposophical Society 1923/1924*
264 *From the History and Contents of the First Section of the Esoteric School, 1904–1914*
266/1 *Aus den Inhalten der esoterischen Stunden. Band 1: 1904–1909*
346 *The Book of Revelation and the Work of the Priest*